We Are the Economy

We Are the Economy

The Buddhist Way of Work, Consumption, and Money

Kai Romhardt, PhD

Translated by Christine Welter and
Teresa van Osdol

Foreword by Thich Nhat Hanh

 **PARALLAX PRESS**

BERKELEY, CALIFORNIA

Parallax Press
P.O. Box 7355
Berkeley, CA
94707

parallax.org

Parallax Press is the publishing division of
Plum Village Community of Engaged Buddhism, Inc.

Originally published in Germany as *Wir sind die Wirtschaft* in 2009.

Translation © 2020 Christine Welter and Teresa van Osdol

Foreword © 2020 Thich Nhat Hanh

Printed in the United States of America

Cover and text design by Joshua Michels

Library of Congress Cataloging-in-Publication Data

Names: Romhardt, Kai, author.
Title: We are the economy : the Buddhist way of work, consumption, and
    money / Kai Romhardt, PhD.
Identifiers: LCCN 2020000120 (print) | LCCN 2020000121 (ebook) | ISBN
    9781946764584 (paperback) | ISBN 9781946764591 (ebook)
Classification: LCC BQ4570.E25 R6613 2020 (print) | LCC BQ4570.E25
    (ebook) | DDC 294.3/373--dc23
LC record available at https://lccn.loc.gov/2020000120
LC ebook record available at https://lccn.loc.gov/2020000121

1 2 3 4 5 / 24 23 22 21 20

Contents

Foreword by Thich Nhat Hanh

In 1999, we offered a mindfulness retreat for business people in Plum Village, our practice center in the Southwest of France. We practiced sitting meditation and enjoyed breathing in and breathing out. We practiced walking meditation, stepping on the earth gently with our feet, arriving with each step in the present moment, and touching the wonders of life. In the retreat, we looked inside of each of us to see how we work, how we deal with financial topics, and how we consume. Can we be successful economically and preserve our mindfulness at the same time? Yes, we can.

We can live peacefully and happily as business people. Even companies and organizations can be peaceful and happy. We want our companies to be successful and flourish, but this doesn't have to happen at the expense of other enterprises. Companies can grow and succeed while supporting each other.

Kai Romhardt spent more than one and a half years as a long-term practitioner in Plum Village. He joined the daily mindfulness practice of our monastic community. In this book Kai shows us how the practices of stopping and deep looking can become a powerful instrument to overcome the suffering caused by our wrong economical thinking and acting. Mindful breathing, walking meditation, deep listening, and kind speech support these efforts.

When we look deeply into our own happiness and suffering, we will see that we don't live separately from the happiness and suffering of others. True happiness is not possible without understanding and compassion. By seeking power, wealth, and sensual pleasure, we can cause a lot of suffering and desperation in others. With the help of mindfulness practice, we can enjoy the present moment and touch the wonders of life within us and around us. We can realize that we have all the conditions in our life that we need to be happy—now, in this very moment.

The insight that happiness is no individual matter and that the well-being of others represents our own well-being will help us to work, consume, and deal with finances in a new way. We will enjoy our own success as well as the success of others. With the help of non-dualistic thinking we can work together to transform our economy.

Thich Nhat Hanh
Plum Village, France, 1999

Preface to the New Edition

When this book was first published, the concept of mindfulness in the economy seemed rather far-fetched. Those times have passed, thank goodness.

This book illustrates how Buddhist teachings and practice can help create a more human economy. The economy is not simply created by those at the top, but rather depends on every single one of us. Everyone is continuously contributing to the daily creation of our economy, either as a consumer, saver, investor, or worker. It is a matter of starting with ourselves and extending our influence outward in concentric circles. Everything depends on our own personal attitudes toward work, consumption, and money.

More and more people have realized that we cannot continue to work with old economic ideas and values. More and more people are questioning our economic principles. Buddhist teachings, the Dharma, help us to reach a new understanding of the economy, an approach that serves the interests of life.

Letting go of previously held mind-sets is a lengthy process. It awakens resistance and can only start with the individual. I experienced this the hard way. Nine years of intense socialization in economic concepts shaped my thinking and the way I interpreted the world. These years clearly left their marks on my mind.

My career in economics started with commercial training at the Axel Springer publishing house. I went on to study business management in Hamburg and St. Gallen and eventually received my PhD in knowledge management in Geneva. I held internships at McKinsey & Company and Roland Berger Consultants, and I also spent intense periods of time with the student organization AIESEC and the Hamburg Business Juniors.

I wrote a management best-seller at age thirty, received an economic research award, and started working as a consultant for McKinsey & Company. Values like performance, competitive thinking, growth, and success dominated my belief system. They were my inner compass. They came as naturally to me as breathing.

Yet I was still not happy. I wasn't even content. Something was wrong. Where was the promised reward for all my efforts? There was no peace, no contentment. After I had climbed a mountain, I saw that there were more mountains, there was always more pressure. I began to doubt the meaning of my career path more and more. These doubts frightened me. In the face of this contradiction, my mind and body finally surrendered.

During the crisis that followed, I questioned all my earlier beliefs. What is it that makes me really happy? What makes me content? What can I do to lead a meaningful life? What is my deepest motivation? What do I see when I look at the world?

I asked myself these questions eighteen years ago. They gave my life and my work a new direction. After intensive seeking and studying, I found the best answers in Buddhist teachings, meditation, and practice. I spent two years in Buddhist practice centers. My concept of self and my thoughts regarding what we call the economy changed extensively. I began to see the true sources of happiness and contentment, and I began to let go of competitive thinking, inner restlessness, and other inner demons. I recognized that we can start the process of transformation in our own mind, that we need to begin within ourselves if we want to change ourselves and our economy. We need to change ourselves if we want to create a more mindful and meaningful economy.

Unless we tame our spirit and continuously work on our minds, we will not be able to transform our attitudes toward consumption, money, and work. Our current attitudes towards consumption, money, and work won't make us happy. On the contrary, they have the power to destroy us and our society.

In this book I want to introduce the components of a "Mindful Economy." An economy that serves life. An economy whose actors strive for clarity and a deep awareness of their actions.

Our perspective on the economy needs to be reexamined. Ruthless self-evaluation, continuous comparisons, latent dissatisfaction, misguided coordinate systems, and false concepts of happiness lie at the heart of the current illusory economic truths. We need to let go of destructive thoughts and actions that stand in the way of straightforward happiness. In hundreds of conversations and discussions, people have told me about their personal transformation that started with a commitment to meditation and mindfulness practice.

Only ten years ago, Buddhism and the economy, meditation and production, compassion and economic success seemed to be worlds apart. They seemed irreconcilable. I was sure that this was not the case. I personally experienced it in my work with the Network for Mindful Business. My main motivation for writing this book was to show the treasure of the Dharma and the transformational power of mindfulness practice. I wanted to see both come alive and apply them to certain business activities.

I was and still am deeply convinced that this kind of change is possible. I witnessed it on a small and a large scale, personally as well as with friends in our Network for Mindful Business. We started meeting in 2004 to deepen our understanding of mindful business activities and to experiment with them. We wanted to fearlessly examine the fundamental pillars of our economic system, to change them and renew them with more wholesome ways of thinking and values. In times of insecurity, crises, and radical changes, the return to the essential, and the renunciation of greed, hatred, and delusion are of the greatest importance.

I notice a great longing to abandon these mental poisons. Working with banks, insurance companies, energy producers, social agencies, NGOs—everywhere I meet people who wish that they themselves and their organization could be freed from unwholesome burdens. I encounter great fear and great courage. Regardless of their profession or academic title, the people I meet all long for the same things: they want more connections, more contentment, more meaning, and more love. They suffer because they feel disconnected from what they perceive as truly important due to the demands of their work. It is wonderful to experience that these connections can be renewed.

Our society is now much more open to the subject of mindfulness in different fields of life. Managers are eager to have their photos taken while meditating, and the number of scientific studies about mindfulness is exploding. Various magazines, institutes, and consulting companies have added the word *mindful* to their corporate name. What kind of change will this movement initiate? Which economic ideas do we need to reexamine? Which apparent economic truths and concepts need to be cast overboard? How profound a change is needed? We know that the change has to start within ourselves. We need to accept that we stand in the way of our own simple happiness.

Right now there is a lot of talk surrounding a secularized version of Buddhism. People are looking for a type of Buddhism detached from its historic connections and terminologies, free of any aspects of religiosity, so that it can more easily tie into our society. The promise that mindfulness leads to greater performance, effectivity, stamina, and stress resistance dominates the discussion. Insight and wisdom, as well as compassion, play a lesser role. The increasing prominence and prevalence of mindfulness allows more and more people to learn about the practice, yet at the same time the depth of the Dharma is more and more simplified. So we need to stay alert that we don't diminish a lifelong path of practice and a life strongly rooted in ethical principles into a simple tool that will help to lift our turbo-capitalism to an even higher level. In my experience we don't do ourselves a favor by trying to surpass ourselves.

In this book I made the conscious decision to name the Buddhist roots that inspired it and to apply the Buddhist terminology. I love the Dharma and I can share this with everyone. I love the depth and immensity of the Dharma's teaching and I am completely aware of the fact that as a Dharma teacher I am still a beginner in many fields of practice.

When people want to hire me for a seminar, a talk, or a workshop, I usually ask: "How Buddhist can it be?" Some classes on the subject of mindfulness are based on the assumption that you can train mindfulness while excluding questions of ethics. This is not possible. My teacher, Thich Nhat Hanh, always emphasizes that mindfulness and ethics are two sides of the same coin. Mindfulness creates a realm that activates our fundamental awakened nature and allows us naturally to act in an ethical way. Ethical actions strengthen our connection with the world and with ourselves. Mindfulness gives us clarity and a compass for wholesome actions.

Organizations that engage in such an in-depth process or implement it in their mission primarily want their members to act more compassionately, and more wisely, gain more understanding, be happier, and find more meaning within the organization. Members should be allowed to develop their true potential. The organization is a means to an end. It serves higher goals for the greater good. It is a beneficial and logical side effect that members of these organizations also begin to act more effectively and live in a more relaxed, healthier manner. This process relies on a mindfulness-based business ethic that provides meaning and direction.

This book seeks to provide clarity. I was surprised by how many different companies and organizations were interested in looking at the potential of mindfulness and its effect on their daily work routines and ethical orientations. While giving talks, and workshops, and conducting training sessions, retreats, and individual coaching sessions with entrepreneurs and individuals, I gained an even deeper insight into the challenges and aspirations of all the different actors within our economic system.

This book also helped the Network for Mindful Business to grow. In many cities in German-speaking countries, we founded regional groups that get together on a regular basis and exchange ideas about mindful working, mindful consumption, and a more wholesome approach in dealing with money and finances. These are the central themes of this book. Group members also support each other on the path of understanding and compassion.

We now have a "Business Sangha," where like-minded individuals can meet to meditate together and to exchange ideas. The network has initiated many publications that build on the ideas of this book. We tested and developed methods and principles together to design our work in organizations in a more beneficial way. We now work with both more ease and more depth. Today the network is a non-profit organization with regional groups in twenty different cities organizing initiatives and planning about 160 events a year.

Through our work in this network over the last few years, we were able to connect central insights from Buddhist teachings with our economic daily life, which we summarized in Buddhist economic ethical principles. We developed a "Mindful Business Commitment" which consists of six practice areas. We offer a ceremony for those who want to accept the commitment as a voluntary obligation and practice. It is a practice-based Hippocratic oath for economically active people. The introduction states:

As I commit to a regular mindfulness practice and to guiding my spirit toward wholesome actions, I make an important contribution to positive changes to our economic system. I receive insights and meaning and I simultaneously nurture my compassion. As I experience the interconnectedness of all beings, my life obtains a clear direction. By looking at economic interrelationships guided by a perspective of mindfulness, I gain a deeper understanding and become the change I want to see in the world. I can begin to sow wholesome seeds, which may change the very core of our economy and society and possibly even heal them.

Only by working together can we create a more mindful economy, whether we are entrepreneurs, heads of households, or small savers. Many of the ideas introduced here need an actual community in order to take root. This book is neither a finished concept, a handbook, nor a to-do-list. It is an invitation to walk a more mindful path by entering an ongoing process to create a more meaningful economy. With this in mind, I hope that the new edition of this book will scatter more seeds of mindfulness out into the world and also encourage us to go forward with humor and clarity, fearlessly and modestly, to observe the seemingly normal with an open spirit and mind.

May all beings be happy!

Kai Romhardt
Berlin, 2017

We Are the Economy

Economic processes permeate our lives. We work. We shop. We borrow money or invest money. Simply by working, consuming, and managing our money, we support and perpetuate everything we refer to as the economy. We are this economy. But does this economy serve our true intentions? Does our current economic system contribute positively to our happiness in life? All human beings long for a sense of community, love, trust, and understanding. Our work, our behavior as consumers, and our money can and should support us in this endeavor. Our common objective should be to foster a meaningful economy that in turn creates more meaning.

Our current version of the economy not only disappoints us—it makes many of us angry. Economic and financial crises create an atmosphere of fear and insecurity. Many companies operate under increased stress, pressure, and competitive thinking. Meaningfulness and joy are not prioritized at work. Excess and greed undermine our trust in the economic elite. How did this happen? What is going wrong? How did we foster an economy that doesn't take care of our deepest needs, that weakens our communities, that increases our fears and discontent and constrains our hearts?

In times of crisis, we feel victimized. We are the victims of greedy investment banks, incompetent politicians, unforgiving market paradigms and cold managers who cut jobs or move them abroad. We seem to be the silent observers of a powerful system that envelops, molds, and restricts us in the form of prices, wages, liabilities, taxes, jobs, and logistics. To resign ourselves to being observers, however, is inaccurate and dangerous. Instead of angrily searching for the culprits and only criticizing the larger structures, we should also focus on what we can do in order to change our economy on macro and micro levels.

The economy doesn't simply happen to us. The economy is not a self-sufficient system that exists beyond our sphere of influence. Nor is it an event that we watch as powerless spectators. We shop, sell, save, and borrow money on a daily basis. We work or we don't. We develop needs that we meet in some way; some of those ways make a meaningful impact, others are harmful. We are either unhappy or happy with our lives. We consume responsibly or excessively, we buy consciously or unconsciously, we support meaningful or senseless endeavors. It can go either way.

Every day we choose anew. Even though larger economic structures hold a good deal of influence, we are freer than we think. This is equally wonderful and challenging. The economy is no hard and steadfast law of nature, but rather the expression of our actual individual and collective spirits. Every day we have the opportunity to move the economy in a more meaningful direction. As we buy and consume more mindfully, invest and borrow more consciously, and work with greater awareness, we create a micro economy that differs greatly from the macroeconomic system.

Millions and billions of these small, medium-size, and larger economic activities can weave, day by day, a new economy and create the potential for positive change.

Mankind produced a different kind of economic behavior in each of its developmental phases. As our attitudes changed, our economy changed. This book invites you to explore a fresh, practical look into core economic issues. Which theories, concepts, and structures can we trust? What kind of an economy do we want?

Toxic Economic Concepts

In our pursuit of happiness as individuals and as a society, we have come to rely on several central economic concepts: economic growth, competition, efficiency, return on investments, rivalry performance, and other ideas have left a deep impression on us. We evaluate ourselves according to these standards. Do these ideas contribute to our happiness?

Fewer and fewer people are accepting the promises of economists, corporate leaders, and politicians: that economic growth, flourishing companies, and rising share prices will guarantee the "good life." Our entire society is ridden with a confidence crisis. If we take a close look, we can recognize the toxic nature of a whole range of economic concepts.

Let's look at the dogma of economic growth. What exactly is growing? What do the markets for (1) antidepressants, (2) prisons, (3) luxury yachts, (4) private security services, and (5) cosmetic surgery have in common? They are growing worldwide. Does this growth contribute to our happiness? I don't think so. As the demand for these goods is growing, we can safely assume that (1) depression, (2) exclusion and violence, (3) extravagance and greed, (4) fear and insecurity, and (5) self-hatred and feelings of inferiority will also increase. Growth in these areas is a symptom of increased spiritual suffering. We don't pay enough attention to these interrelations when we talk about "growth."

Rivalry and competition are regarded as the cardinal virtues of the market economy. Yet competition creates stress, polarization, and tension on all different levels of our society. Competition stresses rivalry instead of cooperation. As we take a deeper look, we recognize that many problems of modern societies, like stress, burnout, depression, and restlessness are fueled by the idea of competition. We can never have enough. We are never secure.

In many areas our economy has been disconnected from our real needs. The economy doesn't make us happier, more content, or compassionate, but instead increases our suffering, nurtures our discontent, and weakens our communities. During the last few decades, we allowed certain economic concepts and ideas to gain too much power over our lives. It is time to tame the monster. But before we can do that, we need to clear our minds.

This book will show alternatives to a number of economic concepts and ideas in its main three chapters. I will challenge the ideas of growth, returns on investment, profit, and success. Our economic thinking is rooted in false presumptions of cause and effect and operates by using toxic terms and hypotheses. Does our current economy help us feel kinder and more content? Most economists believe that these questions lie beyond the realm of their responsibilities. Yet they matter a great deal. They are essential. Any economy that ignores our mental well-being and human potential, and which doesn't attempt to understand and meet our deepest needs, should be replaced with a broader perspective.

A New Model: Mindful Economics

In Buddhism it is said that "It is our spirit that creates our world." Our spirit encompasses our thinking, our feelings, our judgments, and our sensory perceptions. All our ideas, theories, values, and memories are part of our spirit. Our actual state of mind and our moods are determined by how we experience our everyday life and our surroundings. Similarly, we create our economic realities and guide all economic decisions. The roots of happiness, joy, or contentment are also of a spiritual nature. We should obtain a deep clarity about our personal mental processes. We should know how our mind works. Only when we know what we think and feel, how we perceive and understand, will we understand the world on a deeper level and make free decisions. The key to such mental clarity lies in the cultivation of mindfulness.

Mindfulness is the ability of our mind to see the world for what it really is. Mindfulness is not a concept, but rather a state of mind that we can train like any other muscle. I will introduce several effective and tried methods of cultivating this particular state of mind in this book. The great gift of mindfulness is clarity, and we will focus on this clarity and how it can help to revolutionize our thought process regarding economic relations.

Increased mindfulness can provide greater insight into mental processes. We notice what we expect when we buy a new car; we recognize the feeling that sweeps over us when we check our bank account, and feel the tension in our body when we compare ourselves with our colleagues. We explore the deeper motivations behind our actions, carve out the essential, decondition our mind, and create neutral spaces. We observe our emotional expectations when we shop, we feel our agitation when we scrutinize stock prices, and we recognize how we lose our connection to the beautiful present moment due to stress, constant planning, and speculating.

Mindfulness takes us right back to the real world. It connects us with the wonder of the present moment. We live only in this moment. We do not live in the past or in the future. Our life is made up of present moments. If we let the present pass us by, we miss our lives. As soon as we become aware of the present moment, a new door opens.

These realizations change our work habits, our consumption, and our attitudes toward money and finances. We are building on the experiences of hundreds of mindfulness practitioners. Mindfulness is no magic potion, but rather a path of practice. It is a mental tool that will provide a perspective into an inspiring, more meaningful, and more beneficial economy.

The Courage of a Vision

Our current economic system offers us little in terms of inspiration. Except for a few rare, brilliant entrepreneurs, our economy mainly emits stagnation. It scares many of us, and we feel helpless thinking about it. The stock market seems like an unpredictable wild beast that can tear down entire industries and national economies with its unforeseeable fluctuations. This can't be right. We need a different vision. We need the courage to demand a different kind of economy, one we can put to the test little by little in our own lives.

We need the heart, the discipline, and the personal experience to organize our economic processes in a more meaningful, mindful, and caring way. Then we will find the strength to draft and live an inspiring economic vision.

How would we live in an economy that:

- doesn't scare us;
- serves rather than enslaves us, and isn't an end in itself;
- increases our mental well-being;
- makes us more content instead of increasing our discontent;
- respects and cherishes our livelihoods, instead of ruining them;
- insists on moderation instead of wastefulness;
- integrates ethics;
- brings people together instead of separating them;
- feeds our true needs instead of creating artificial and unwholesome desires;
- strengthens our mind instead of exploiting it;
- is motivated by moderation, gratitude, happiness, and trust rather than by greed, dissatisfaction, envy, and distrust;
- is led by wise leaders and role models who operate on the basis of universal ethical principles?

This is the vision we need to adopt, instead of the status quo. We need patience, discipline, and trustworthy companions on this journey. We also need to experience how our work and all other economic processes gradually become true sources of happiness, joy, connection, and other positive mental states. The foundation for this change is a realistic, development-oriented, and positive understanding of what it truly means to be a human being.

A New Concept of Man

With *Homo economicus* (a term first used by critics of John Stuart Mill to describe humans as actors who are consistently rational and efficient in pursuing their own self-interest), economists created a negative and unrealistic reference model for the human being. No one has ever met a human who acted like a rational machine, maximizing benefits for his or her own interests and operating according to a fixed set of preferences based on full and complete information. Today you would be hard-pressed to find a living economist who would accept *Homo economicus* as a realistic concept. Yet this artificial construct, this fictional character, continues to inhabit economic textbooks, theories, and formulations of central economic cause-effect relationships.

Psychology, philosophy, sociology, and other sciences have shown in many ways that the *Homo economicus* is an inappropriate, flawed model of man. For thousands of years, all our best thinkers have been discussing human nature. How do human beings actually function? What motivates them? Every one of us has a wealth of experience in this field—with ourselves and with each other. Are humans good or evil by nature, free or self-determined, driven by instinct or capable of rational decisions, a child of God or an accumulation of cells?

This book most closely follows the image of human beings found in Buddhism. During his very intense process of self-examination and meditation, the historical Buddha gained central insights into human nature. These insights became the basis for his teachings, the Dharma. The Buddha's experiences were confirmed by countless meditators, Dharma teachers, monks, and nuns as well as lay practitioners for over 2,500 years. This is an unprecedented empirical test in which millions of people individually confirmed the image of human beings that the Buddha himself had arrived at. Which other actual theory do we know of that has been confirmed by each generation of scientists for over 2,500 years? Is there any other idea of humankind that has been scrutinized by such an extensive investigation process? This comprehensive historical foundation in a living practice warrants a closer look at the Buddhist image of the human being and its relevance for our times and our economy.

What were the insights of the historical Buddha? He realized that our true nature is boundless love, compassion, and wisdom. He recognized that we can clear our mind, through practice, so deeply that we are able to understand our true nature, the nature of interbeing and the reciprocal interconnectedness of all life. He recognized that all processes of human existence are forever changing, and that any attachment to and identification with an immutable self results in countless problems. Through patient practice, we are able to clear and sharpen our mind so that our wonderful, radiant, and true nature begins to shine more and more.

You might be skeptical on reading this. It took me years of cultivating mindfulness to gain a deeper trust in this understanding of humankind. As I related to the bright nature of my counterparts instead of expecting them to act like calculating egoists, a lot changed. It is time to retire the term *Homo economicus* and all its relatives.

During his lifetime, the Buddha was recognized as an enlightened being. This doesn't remotely mean that he was supernatural, but that he fully realized his human potential and illuminated it.

Economy of Abundance Instead of Economy of Scarcity

Our economy starts with an assumption of scarcity. The more we have and possess, the more we perceive things to be insufficient. Despite substantial technical progress and material improvements, we still want more. We are materially better off than any generation before us, yet we suffer from a spiritual hunger. This hunger can't simply be alleviated by more innovation in the area of product or service development.

During every moment of every day, our spirit is in a specific state. Sometimes we are impatient and stressed. Other times we are happy and relaxed. The total sum of these small moments forms our days, weeks, months, years, and eventually our lives. If we want to develop a positive direction for our life, we need to let go of problematic conditions and not only strengthen wholesome states of mind within, but also anchor these in our lives. We are usually aware which states of mind are enriching our lives and which ones destroy us in the long run. Which of the following states of mind do you want to see flourishing in your life, and which ones would you rather let go of?

mindfulness · anger · acceptance · anxiety

tension · modesty · gratefulness · depression

jealousy · joy · fearlessness · patience · serenity

happiness · greed · doubt · distrust · contentment

inner restlessness · envy · wisdom · concentration

distrust · compassion · self-hatred · self-love

pride · poor concentration · unhappiness · trust

In my seminars at St. Gallen University, my students always readily agreed on the states of mind they wanted to encourage in their lives. They did not want to be governed by anger, discontent, and greed. They wished for more trust and calm. But they were not quite sure how to strengthen the positive states of mind and how to weaken the unwholesome ones. This is difficult—we live in an environment that encourages dissatisfaction, competition, and "nothing is ever good enough" on a daily basis.

What we are looking for and perceive to be missing is already within us. We can't find it externally by choosing to consume, accelerating our career, or accumulating other successes that count in a competitive society. When we cultivate mindfulness, we realize that we live in a world of abundance. Then we can focus less on the material dimensions of our lives and strengthen the spiritual dimensions of our being, which are crucial for our quality of life.

The assumption that the most important goods required to fulfill our needs are limited is one of the greatest fallacies of our market economy. This might be true for material goods. The goods, however, that determine our deeper well-being in prosperous societies are of an immaterial nature. Love, meaning, happiness, peace, joy, contentment, and other states of mind are all immaterial. These "goods" are infinitely available to our mind. They lead the economic logic *ad absurdum*. They will never be acquired by economic principles. Love, joy, peace, and happiness are in no way limited goods we can buy, permanently own, or accumulate. It is up to us to touch on these mental treasures again and again. Mindfulness plays a very important role in this scenario. A true smile is priceless. It is given freely and thrives on spreading its positive resonance.

When we discuss mindful economic activity, we aren't referring to an economy that satisfies superficial, endless needs, but rather to an economy that helps us cultivate joy, happiness, and contentment on a deeper, spiritual level. Our actual economic system has failed us in this regard. Decades of growth haven't made us any more content, joyful, or happy. Many scientific surveys and studies agree on this fact.

The things that our inner souls most desire, the most valuable things in life, are limitlessly available and are free. This is a revolutionary statement, so let's say it again: The most valuable matters in our life are available in unlimited quantities and have no monetary value.

Spiritual Growth as a Matter of Priority

A deep understanding of the spiritual dimensions of our lives helps us to see through false promises. Greed will always be greed, and an economy that emphasizes greed and desire has the power of harming us in a serious way. It might even destroy us. Mindfulness helps us to see the connection between economic and mental processes in a new light. In the chapter "We Are the Work," we will examine these processes in detail and introduce strategies to transform them. Right now, it suffices to recognize the enormous importance of the spiritual dimension of all our economic actions, no matter which economic role we take on and which contexts or activity areas we inhabit.

We measure every possible pillar in our economy: revenues and expenses, profits and losses, investments, consumer spending, the gross national product, rates of return, and so on. What we truly need, however, is a mental balance sheet to give us feedback on how we have been developing our spiritual treasures, like joy, happiness, and contentment. How about the chance that a pedestrian on a main street in Zürich, or New York, will receive a smile from a passerby? Did the likelihood of sharing that smile increase or decrease during the last ten years? How can it be that there is only one country in the world that records the changes of mental well-being in the form of a gross happiness product, and takes this measurement seriously (that country is the Kingdom of Bhutan)? Couldn't our comprehensive statistical methods help us to reflect a sophisticated mental image of our society? We need a clear understanding of the development of our collective mind. We need to understand which practices we want to cultivate and which we want to discourage. We should stop our undifferentiated chatter about economic growth. That applies to ourselves as well. A truly successful life requires a happiness compass and the emotional wisdom to see how our life develops. We have to know what it is that grows and shrinks.

Mental Formation	Year 1	Year 2	Change
compassion	●●●○○	●●○○○	↓
joy	●○○○○	●●●○○	↑↑
contentment	●●●○○	●●●●○	↑
gratitude	●●●○○	●●●○○	
fear/insecurity	●●●○○	●●●●○	↑
anger/rage/aggression	●●●○○	●●●○○	
depression	●●○○○	●●●●○	↑↑
desire/greed	●●●○○	●●●○○	

Illustration 1: Balance sheet of different mental formations

The true potential for growth won't be found in untapped markets, but within ourselves. It is of a spiritual and immaterial nature. We need to question our economic activities—do they contribute to spiritual growth, or reinforce unwholesome mental formations? There is no need to glorify products, companies, and industries that rely on spiritual exploitation or crises to build their material growth. It makes much more sense to unite in supporting processes, institutions, and people who carry wholesome and meaningful seeds in the world.

We should work together to recognize and transform the unwholesome mental formations that take root in our economic structures, and companies, and in our own minds. We should emphasize the mental formations as well as their potential for change:

- Greed is the problem rather than the greedy individual.

- Inertia is the problem rather than the lethargic individual.

- Discontent is the problem rather than the ever dissatisfied individual.

- Aggression is the problem rather than the aggressive individual.

- Dishonesty is the problem rather than dishonest people.

All of us carry the seeds of greed, laziness, discontent, aggression, and dishonesty within ourselves. Greed doesn't live outside of us in boardrooms and on executive floors. It lives inside all of us. We truly aren't that different from those we consider to be our enemies.

The Approach of This Book
This is certainly not an all-encompassing book "about" the economy. Plenty of abstract analyses in that vein have been published. This book deals with our own personal and collective stories and how we can create the economy that we desire. It is important that we start small. The three main chapters of the book introduce and examine the central areas of action I am referring to when I discuss mindful economic activity: work, money and finance, and consumption. We will ask ourselves a practical question: How can we approach these concepts differently to lead to a more meaningful, more aware, and more fulfilled life? Our focus is on our daily economic transactions: our actions at work, our daily purchases, or our thoughts about possible financial investments. We will examine the central areas of work, money, and consumption systematically, looking at four dimensions:

1. "How?": Which mental qualities and effective forces are intrinsic to our actions? What is their fragrance? How do I act when I work, when I deal with money, and when I consume? What is my mental attitude when engaging in economic activity? For example: Do I work in an irritable or joyful manner?

2. "What?": What is the true nature of work, money, and consumption? Do I have enough transparency and comprehension in these areas? What do I perceive as "normal"? What are the basic beliefs that guide my actions? For example: How is my money invested? Do I understand the activities of my bank, and do I support them?

3. "How much?": What are the relations of my consumption to other areas of life and living environments? Do I strike the right balance? When is enough enough? For example: When have I eaten enough?

4. "Why?": What drives me? What is my deepest motivation? What gives meaning to my life? Example: How do I define success?

It is possible to do the right thing (what?) when handling money, work, and consumption in a wholesome way (how?), in the right measure (how much?), and for sensible reasons (why?). It is also possible, however, to act in unwholesome ways, using destructive behavior motivated by vain and harmful causes. We need to be highly attentive if we want to steer the right course in this endeavor. The following illustration explains the structure of the three main chapters.

Dimensions of Actions	Subject Areas: Work	Money/Finances	Consumption
Fragrance (How?)	What is my state of mind when I work? What effect does my work have on me?	How do I deal with money? How are my interactions with money reflected in my spirit?	What is my state of mind when I consume? What effect does consumption have on me?
Genuine nature (What?)	What is the essence of my work? What did I choose?	Where do I invest? Do I understand my finances?	What do I consume? Do I understand the object of consumption?
Appropriateness (How much?)	How much do I work? Are the ratios acceptable?	How much money do I make and how much do I own? When is enough enough?	How much do I consume? Do I live in moderation?
Motivation (Why?)	What is my deepest motivation for working?	What is my deepest motivation for interacting with money and finances?	Why do I consume? What triggers my consumption?

Illustration 2: Subject areas and dimensions of actions

Mindfulness shows us, in concrete ways, which paths lead to a more meaningful, more sustainable economy that serves the interests of life. Our first goal is to change the economy in small ways. As we change our work practices, consume more mindfully, and deal more consciously with money, we make small waves within our economic system. These waves add up and may create a movement that can revolutionize our ways of economic thinking and acting.

We Are the Work

How, where, and for whom do we work? What contributions does our work make? What does our work mean to us? Does our work make sense?

What does work mean to us? What do we expect of it? When does it bring us joy? When does it make us anxious? Did we choose our work, or did it find us? What is its fragrance? Do we smile when we drive to work? Are we happy when our workday is over?

Work is of great importance in our society. Unless we are among close friends, our work often determines how we are perceived. Our profession and position play an important role for our self-image and identity. So many of us spend the larger part of our conscious lifetime working. When we ask ourselves, "Who am I?" our answer is usually: "I am a physician," "I am a fashion designer," "I am a manager," "I am retired," or "I am unemployed."

We expect a lot from our work. It is supposed to bring us happiness, joy, and meaning. It is supposed to provide us with feelings of security, belonging, and recognition. And of course we expect our work to generate enough money to lead an enjoyable life.

Many of our expectations of our work are quite unrealistic. It's similar to our romantic notions of love. We assume that it is our partner who is responsible for our happiness. Our work won't make us happy. We need to look at our own capacity for happiness. How do we achieve this?

My inflated expectations regarding my work depleted it of joy for many years. Work was a really serious thing for me, something that was hard, even anxiety-provoking. Work was connected to fighting. My expectations of myself and of my work were extremely high.

Work without obvious, outward success was a catastrophe. These work patterns eventually led me into burnout and depression. I realized that I had to reexamine my fundamental attitude toward work.

What Precisely Is My Field of Work?

For the last twenty years I have worked for many different companies performing a variety of tasks. Yet I didn't realize what work in its essence meant to me until I spent time in Plum Village, Thich Nhat Hanh's monastery in southwestern France. It was there that I had the opportunity to experience my work patterns over two years in more than 500 "work meditations." I worked as a car washer, construction worker, choir director, moderator, harvester, driver, handyman, cook, warehouse manager, painter, meditation hall coordinator, garbage collector, organizer, caregiver, shopper, translator, toilet cleaner, and foreman. In short, I wore many different hats.

I let go of many of the certainties I held about work during these diverse activities. Every workday held a new lesson for me. I could see that there was not much of a correlation between my experience of the work and the work itself—it was my mind that colored my activities. On the days I felt irritated, even the most pleasant task felt like an annoyance. On a day when my mood was joyful, I could even paint walls, one of my least favorite tasks, with a smile.

It was a huge relief, a letting go of inner and outer ballast. It felt like a destruction of many of my personal myths about work. After my return to society, the dimensions of my work life changed tremendously.

I would never have thought that our opinion of work is influenced and limited by so many inner and outer forces. I realized how much freedom we can gain when we start to observe mindfully and look deeply into our work conviction and habits.

Let's look closely at the four central dimensions of our work and begin to see how we can reach more meaningful attitudes toward work.

Four Dimensions of Action within Our Work

We will examine the mental dimension, the fragrance, and the radiance of our work as well as our internal attitude and creative impact. How do we work? Do we start our day with a smile or with clenched teeth? It's not what we say but how we say it. Two people can perform the exact same work yet perceive it completely differently. Our mental attitude has an impact on every task we perform. Our customers, coworkers, and supervisors will reflect back upon us the energy that we project. We can start here to understand and change the radiance of our work in concrete steps.

We ask ourselves about the true nature of our work. What am I doing here? What impact does my work have on myself, my environment, and the world? We take a fresh look at our work. We question myths and buzzwords of the working life. We identify the dimensions in which we have a choice or where we have chosen already. Our insights reward us with clarity and the strength to let go of societal standards so we can pave our own path.

We check on our work-life balance. Do we feel exhausted after work? Does our work dominate all other areas of life? Can we relax? Could it be that we aren't challenged enough, and fight against dullness and lethargy? The pace of work has increased consistently in many fields. We can only keep up a concentrated drive if it is balanced with relaxation; activity needs non-activity. Creativity without idleness and maturation ends in a stage of exhaustion all too quickly.

We look at the underlying motivation for our work. What work means for us has a lot to do with how we were formed by the "work history" in our family of origin, societal work norms, and our individual experiences. We need to stop pretending and ask absolutely honestly what we expect from our work. What drives us? What paralyzes us? Whose judgment counts to us and why is that so? What kind of psychological rewards do we gain from work? We will show that classic motivations and motivational training may mislead us.

What do we want to prove to ourselves and to everyone else? What do we expect of our professional career? We will see that it depends on the quality of our underlying motivation whether our work makes us happy or unhappy. The key to a healthy and meaningful relationship to work lies within ourselves.

The Fragrance of Work

How do I work? Which mental states do I cultivate in my work? How does my work affect my environment? What is the fragrance of my work environment?

How we experience our work depends only partially on our work environment. Two people may experience the same situation very differently. It all depends on our state of mind. As long as we are irritable and aggressive, even a minor challenge may throw us off. If we feel relaxed and peaceful, however, we can manage difficult experiences without too much effort.

In Buddhism, we say that all things arise out of the spirit. As soon as this notion becomes a fully felt experience, our perspective on the world changes dramatically. We pay closer attention to how our present perspective colors our experience. We pay more attention to the "How" of every activity. We realize that it is not just good food, for instance, that makes us happy, but also the way in which we eat that can lead to happiness.

Each of our activities carries a certain fragrance. Picture two train conductors at work. They check tickets, give advice, answer questions, and deal with disgruntled travelers. The quality and effect of these activities depends to a high degree on the mental state of the conductor. If they radiate joy, equanimity, and concentration, their activities will meet with a similar response. If they make their way through the train in a visibly angry fashion, with irritability and unfriendliness, then their environment will reflect back the same mental states.

Buddhist philosophy distinguishes between wholesome and

unwholesome mental states. Wholesome mental states—or spiritual treasures—help us to connect with the world. Unwholesome mental states—or spiritual plagues—disconnect us from ourselves and from the world. Examples of wholesome mental states are trust, empathy, joy, and contentment. Examples of unwholesome mental states are greed, anger, pride, and envy.

Each of these mental states rests as a sleeping seed in the depths of our consciousness—also called "store consciousness" in Buddhist psychology. It lies there waiting for an external impulse that will awaken it and allow it to rise up and shape our mind consciousness. When a seed of joy arises because we meet an old friend, we experience joy.

The more we touch wholesome states of mind, the more these will grow, become stronger, and manifest themselves. Over time our store consciousness will change. If we can stay in touch with positive seeds over a course of time, equanimity might give way to a deep inner calm and eventually even lead to unwavering peace.

Spiritual Treasures ⬆	wisdom	generosity	trust
	compassion	shared joy	gratefulness
	loving kindness	fearlessness	happiness
	contentment	inner freedom	joy
Spiritual Plagues ⬇	fear	pride	jealousy
	anger	lethargy	greed
	discontent	restlessness	ill will
	envy	egoism	ignorance

Illustration 3: Wholesome and unwholesome mental states

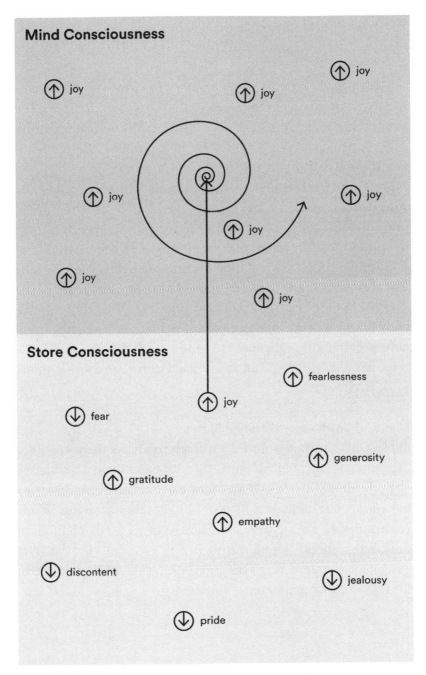

Illustration 4 : Rise of a mental state into the mind consciousness

When unwholesome seeds persist, however, latent irritability may produce strong anger, eventually leading to blind rage and even hatred.

The immaterial treasure of a person, a company, and even a society is the quality of the seeds in the store consciousness. The stronger the seed in the store consciousness, the more it will influence the person carrying it and their environment. It is important to take good care of this garden of consciousness.

We should refrain from finding fault with our colleagues, superiors, coworkers, and clients when it is us who spread unwholesome mental states with a negative fragrance. It is up to us to become aware of our own fragrance and begin to change it. Mindfulness gives us the ability to accomplish this. Therefore, the first step is: "I know what fragrance I spread. I am aware of the energy I radiate." I am aware of my impatience. I accept responsibility for my mental fragrance and admit that continued anger will have negative consequences in my life. With this attitude, I take responsibility for my mind and will act more consciously in my work environment.

Effects of Unwholesome Mental States

There are days when work feels like a burden, yet there are other days when we accomplish our tasks with ease. Some days we face obstacle after obstacle, and on other days the whole world seems to support our endeavors. It could be that the cause lies in our environment. In most cases, however, the cause for these different work experiences is found within, in our own state of mind. If we struggle with our work, we are often under the impact of one of the following mental states:

Unwholesome Mental State	Negative Effects on Our Work
irritability	conflicts, wrong perceptions, compromised communication
anxiety	reduced intelligence, selective perspective
jealousy	diminished cooperation, separation, waste of energy
poor concentration	mistakes, waste of time, misunderstandings
inattention	unconscious work behavior, no access to deeper dimension of our work, accidents (physical, emotional, verbal), ambiguous motivation
anger and rage	escalated conflicts, violence, tunnel vision, dissemination of fear, separation
discontent	tension, beauty goes unnoticed, flawed defect orientation, negativity, jealousy, conflicts
greed	dishonesty, excess, inconsiderateness
lethargy	procrastination, diminished energy, ineffectiveness, missing conclusions, paralysis of one's environment
restlessness	stress, contagious nervousness, tension, danger of burnout, destruction of collective concentration
pride	hubris, disconnection from environment, incorrect perception of cause-and-effect relationships

Table 1: Unwholesome mental states and their possible effects on our work

Many employees suffer from work-related anxieties. This fear colors our workdays and is reflected back to us. It leads to burnout, depression and stress, mistrust, irritability, pride, and impatience. Jealousy and envy also contaminate joyful productive workdays. These mental states take away our ability to connect in a positive way with our environment, to cooperate and perceive all parameters of our work clearly. In the long term they will likely make us physically sick, and in any case they will make us unhappy.

Mindfulness helps us to recognize our present state of mind. We shouldn't permit negative states of mind to rule our working days.

Work Meditation: What Am I Really Doing?

Work meditation, I have found, is the most effective method to connect with our state of mind related to the work we do. During the last five years, I have offered about twenty seminars in which we used work meditation to get to a state of self-awareness. Zen Master Hakuin says: "Meditation in the midst of activity is a thousand times superior to meditation in stillness."

We choose simple activities for work meditation (cutting vegetables, sweeping, washing dishes). We take plenty of time in order to slow down our habitual work tempo. Slowing down helps us to see more clearly what we are actually doing and what we experience. While we are working, we stay closely in contact with our breath and focus completely on the activity that we are performing. We can use mindfulness bells to interrupt our work period, reminding us to stay focused. We practice: pause, breathe, smile. If we practice in this way, we can reach a high form of mindfulness and consciousness during work meditation. Here are a few statements from people I have done working meditation with:

My task was so simple—to cut carrots. Yet I felt it was stressful. No one really expected me to do it a certain way, yet I felt this enormous pressure and impatience within. I wanted to get done with the work as soon as possible. While doing the work, it seemed impossible to relax. There was no way to deny it: this pressure was something I created myself.

All of a sudden I realized that no one was forcing me to work carelessly.

I gained valuable insights for my work life in a communal bathroom in France. Cleaning toilets? This job always belonged to those that I needed to avoid. During work meditation, I became aware of my inner resistance. My face tensed up again and again. I would pause, then breathe in slowly three times, and tried, as it had been suggested, to smile toward the toilet bowl. It seemed so ridiculous at first, but it helped! During my four work meditations, I learned that it is possible to work in a toilet with joy. During the work I realized how incredibly powerful the matter of "How" is while performing an activity.

Favorable States of Mind in Our Work

We will now examine the effect of some wholesome mental states on our work. Along with cultivating mindfulness at work, we will also focus on the effects and cultivation of concentration, empathy, and joy during our work routine.

Mindfulness: The Royal State of Mind

We will start with the fragrance of mindfulness. There is nothing more important than being focused exactly on what we are doing. In this very moment. We tend to give way too much mental energy to the future and to the past, and we miss the present.

We might be speaking with a customer while already contemplating a contract that hasn't been awarded yet. We are not completely present and in danger of missing the essential of our client's explanations. If we don't succeed in coming back to the present, we are building castles in the air, and our energy gets lost.

Here are some of the effects that mindfulness can have on our everyday working life:

- Mindfulness has no routine—every second is fresh and new. If we are completely present, we learn automatically without great efforts.

- Mindfulness makes us more sensitive toward even the smallest changes in conversations, in meetings, and within ourselves.

- Mindfulness helps us to understand the emotional dimensions of a situation, so we can intervene skillfully.

- Mindfulness connects us with our environment.

- Mindfulness helps us to economize our energy.

- Mindfulness reminds us to pause when we are ruled by unwholesome states of mind.

- Mindfulness helps prevents conflicts and emotional entanglements.

Strong presence changes every situation. Phil Jackson, the most successful basketball coach in NBA history, said that he kept encouraging the Lakers to stay in the present moment and to practice mindfulness. This method constituted the team's success. It was crucial not to plan ahead too much, but to touch the unique nature of each moment in the basketball game. In this state, his players touched "the zone," a state where they didn't try to chase the game, but played gracefully while finding unity and mental presence as a team, which is far superior to any plan or strategy.

Concentration: The Penetrating and Clarifying State of Mind
Concentration is a close friend of mindfulness. While mindfulness allows us to connect with the fullness of the present moment, concentration is the ability to keep our attention focused on one object for a certain amount of time. Buddhists also speak of a "one-pointedness" of the mind. If we can stay completely focused, despite distractions and interruptions, we hold the key to success and self-determination in many demanding professions.

When we concentrate, we consciously decide to stay with one activity and stay the course. The opposite states of concentration are distraction and dispersal—we don't finish tasks or we don't tackle them with the right intensity. Concentration holds many advantages for our work life:

- Concentration allows us to penetrate a problem or situation more deeply.

- Concentration increases the intensity with which we engage in our work.

- Concentration protects against distraction.

- Concentration allows us to prioritize.

Shunryu Suzuki puts it this way: "In calmness there should be activity; in activity there should be calmness."[1]

Concentration does have a dark side, however. Let me give an example from work meditation:

There are a large number of dishes to wash. After all the plates and bowls have been washed, the dish-washing person grabs the electric mixer and washes it carefully in the sink. The device is ruined because it doesn't take water well.

This is an example of false concentration, when we block out everything and concentrate on one task only. We lose sight of the entirety of the situation and therefore invite dire consequences. We ruin the mixer. We concentrate completely on our work and neglect our family. We get caught up in one aspect of a project, and lose sight of its complexity. Concentration and mindfulness need to go hand in hand.

Compassion: The Loving State of Mind

One of the most wonderful and effective states of mind that humans are able to generate is compassion. The quality of compassion is

1. Shunryu Suzuki, *Zen Mind, Beginner's Mind* (Boulder, CO: Shambhala, 2010).

seen as the ultimate goal in Buddhism and a fundamental attitude
to aspire to in all situations and challenges of life. Compassion
(karuna) describes the intent and ability to lessen and transform
suffering within ourselves and others.

People like the Dalai Lama or the Nobel laureate Muhammad
Yunus embody this ability. Their simple presence enables them to
affect their environment in a healing way. As they understand and
accept those they work with, they are able to connect when others
might separate. When we cultivate compassion, all our activities
become favorable.

We love it when we encounter people who deeply understand
our problems, who neither judge nor condemn. These are people
who emanate true warmth. Managers and leaders can have an enormous impact in this area—they have a responsibility to do so. The
Dalai Lama writes: "The people appointing [an executive] should
keep this in the back of their minds at all times: this person will
be responsible for providing the company with a strong and warm
heart. Can he or she do that?"[2]

Are we ready to forgive, to cooperate, and to begin anew? Burnout,
stress, resignation, and conflicts with supervisors are symptoms of
the loss of compassion in many work environments.

Joy: The State of Mind that Connects

If we experience joy in our work, time flies. When we smile, it is
much easier to connect with those around us. It is important to
find joy within ourselves during our day-to-day business life. The
following is an example of an employee:

> *I realized that it is important to actively engage my joy. I am tired
> of getting caught up in the bad or even aggressive vibe of my work
> environment. On my way to work I make a point to smile at the
> bus driver, and the new passengers entering the bus, and I send*

---

2. The Dalai Lama, *The Leader's Way* (New York: Broadway Books, 2009).

*good thoughts to everyone I encounter. I refuse to get caught up
in the sour mood of the early-morning subway riders. When I feel
that someone's anger gets to me, I focus on a natural object of
joy: the lilac in bloom or a small child making eye contact with
me are good examples. This is how I enter the office. I check on a
regular basis whether I've kept a small smile on my face. Whenever I remember my smile, I sense that I am doing good for myself
and my coworkers.*

There is no need to wait for the perfect surroundings that will allow
us to experience joy. We can start with a smile and set the mood for
ourselves and others.

Effects of Wholesome States of Mind

It is impossible to separate our activities from the states of mind
we inhabit when we engage in them. When we perform our work
mindfully, with concentration, compassion, and joy, we will see the
impact. It will manifest clearly. We will have fewer conflicts, we will
notice more important details, our relationships will improve, trust
will increase, and we will be able to help more effectively and understand problems more deeply and comprehensively. Who would
choose to work with an unmindful, distracted, cold, and grumpy
person? Who would want to be characterized like that? Therefore,
we need to attend to the cultivation of the following wholesome
states of mind.

Many people suffer from their work because they only experience
a few wholesome states of mind during a day of work. They may
ask themselves: "What can I do? Our supervisors aren't mindful,
but rather are hectic and aggressive. They show little compassion.
What can I do as an individual?" It is hard to stay constructive
in a destructive environment. A first step is to examine our own
perception carefully, to recognize whether we feed on judgments,
emotions, and tensions in our daily interactions. We can change

that. We can train our mind. It is possible to nourish the wholesome and to starve the unwholesome. If we come to realize that we still can't influence our destructive work environment, we should look for a better one. It is our responsibility to care for our mind. In the following pages we will introduce certain work principles and methods that help to stay on track.

State of Mind	Positive Effects on Our Work
mindfulness	awareness of central factors regarding a certain situation, clear perception, letting go of prejudice, objective thinking, freshness
concentration	getting things done, concentration on the essential
compassion	heartfelt connection with our environment, understanding, empathy, solidarity, cooperation
joy	ease, connection with our environment, personal motivation
patience	avoiding blind actions and short-term thinking
contentment	less stress, more enjoyment and gratitude
fearlessness	freedom, honesty, clear vision, courage to name unpleasant facts
generosity	investment in the future, joy of giving, creating value in sharing
gratefulness	connecting with other players and influences, appreciation of the work of others
humility	avoidance of unrealistic self-image, keeping an eye on the whole picture

Table 2: Wholesome states of mind and their possible effects on our work

Methods of Mindfulness Training

Mindful Breathing: Uniting Body and Mind

Human beings reach their highest cognitive faculty when mind and body work together as one. When we train our mind and body to act in unity, we naturally develop a higher ability to be present, responsive, and clear. Reason and rational thinking can only penetrate one segment of a complex situation. Gut instinct, intuition, and emotional intelligence require direct contact with our bodies.

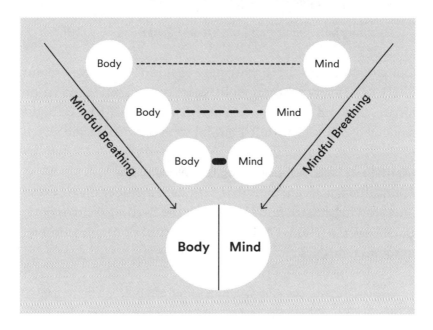

Illustration 5: Bringing body and mind together

During the course of the workday, mind and body keep drifting apart. As we sit at our computer, our thoughts wander and we often forget to take care of our body. We attend meetings and daydream about our next vacation. We walk through town, talk on the phone to clients, and ignore our surroundings as well as our steps and our breath.

Mindful breathing can help us to keep body and mind in unison during all our activities and to stay awake. Even if we assign only a part of our attention to the breath while we are at work, we transform the activity. Give it a try. Sit up straight and take three deep breaths. Try to do this consciously, but also in a relaxed way. Smile at yourself kindly. Hold this book in both hands, and feel the contact between the cover and your hands. Try to follow your breath while reading.

Breathing in, I know that I am breathing in.

Breathing out, I know that I am breathing out.

Can you notice a shift in your state of mind? When we use our breath as an anchor for mindfulness, we create a solid foundation for presence and awareness. Our breath is always with us. Until the moment of our last breath, it is our constant companion and refuge.

Mindfulness Bells: A Pause during Our Working Day
Mindfulness bells are tools that help us remember that it is our intention to practice mindfulness. In the Berlin practice center Quelle des Mitgefühls (Wellspring of Compassion) a practitioner introduced this practice in the following way:

When you arrive, you might hear the sound of a bell, and the people around you will suddenly pause and stop talking and moving. It could be the sound of a phone, the strike of a clock, or the toll of the monastery bell. These are our mindfulness bells. When we hear the sound of the bell, we relax our body and take note of our breath. We do so with ease and joy, without any solemnity or tension. When we hear the sound of the bell we interrupt our conversations and whatever we are doing to turn our attention to the breath. The sound of the bell, has called us: "Please listen; this wonderful sound will take you back to your true home."

This regular interruption of our routine is powerful and lets us reconnect with the reality right in front of us. In the dynamic of a workday, when we begin to feel tired or succumb to a bad mood, the bell helps us to refresh and opt against giving in to negativity or unconsciousness. The mindfulness bell is a reminder, a signal, a friendly push toward mindfulness. I grant myself three mindful breaths and collect myself.

An excellent mindfulness bell is our phone. We can pause when it rings, use it as a conscious stop, and take three mindful breaths instead of immediately picking up and answering. We can also install a mindfulness program on our computer. I use one when I spend long hours on the computer. It reminds me in freely defined intervals with a bell (or a similar sound) to pause for a brief time. At the same time, a window pops up on my screen where I can read the motto of my week.

Red lights, a creaking door, church bells, the trees outside our window, or even the sound of a leaving bus can be used as mindfulness bells. I give out sticky dots in my seminars. We stick them on objects or places where we tend to lose our mindfulness. Some favorites are refrigerator doors, the power button on a laptop, remote controls on different devices, the espresso maker, our phone, or our credit cards. When we work with mindfulness bells, we build natural small pauses into our days that help to calm down our thoughts and keep negative emotions from taking over.

Walking Meditation: Mindful Walking

For me, walking meditation is the most effective and remarkable of all the different mind training methods that I have yet encountered. Walking meditation changed my life. It taught me that every step, every moment of my life holds its own intrinsic value and dignity. Every moment in our life makes its inevitable impact.

We can walk angrily or in a relaxed manner. We can be in a go-go mood or free of worries while we walk. We can be upright or bent, conscious or unconscious, happy or sad. Our life is the sum of many small steps. Walking meditation teaches us that it is up to us to decide the quality of our steps. We relax our body, follow our breath, and synchronize our steps with the in-breath and the out-breath. The monks of Plum Village describe the spirit of walking meditation in the following way:

> *We walk just for walking. We walk with freedom and solidity, no longer in a hurry. We are present with each step. And when we wish to talk, we stop moving or pause and give our full attention to the other person, to which words we choose, and to fully listening.*

Our steps reflect our current state of mind with surprising accuracy. We can start anew with every step and cultivate a wholesome mental formation. Anyone can practice walking meditation just about anywhere. Walking meditation is by no means a technique practiced solely in exceptional situations or alone in the woods. By walking mindfully, we are able to empower concentration and mindfulness as well as regain our freedom in the midst of daily work routines. It is sufficient to reduce our regular walking speed by 20 percent and breathe mindfully. Practicing in this way, we won't attract any attention.

When we get up angrily from our desk in order to attend a meeting, it is helpful to take just a few mindful steps to ground ourselves and attract positive energies. We will arrive at the meeting in a different mood. There lies the power, the effectiveness, and the miracle of walking meditation.

Mindful Listening

Have you ever been in a roundtable meeting where no one truly listens? One person talks while the others look absent-minded and communicate resistance or lack of interest through their postures. How about business meetings where participants are texting, writing emails, and engaging in parallel conversations? These unfocused types of communication bring our energy levels down. We don't feel connected. When there is no contact between speaker and listener, the natural, clear transfer of information breaks down. Our understanding becomes fragmented, and misunderstandings are inevitable.

To support the practice of deep listening, I use a tried and tested tool in my workshops. Before I start a seminar, a lecture, or a retreat, I ring a small bell. The sound of the bell invites listeners to relax, to follow their breath and get more deeply in touch with themselves. The sound of the bell reminds us that we want to listen to each other.

When we listen to a talk, I recommend refraining from thinking about its content too much; simply keep listening. By thinking too much about what we hear, we create a parallel talk in our mind, a talk that judges, comments, speculates, and associates while separating us from our lecturer. I also recommend listening without too much effort, and remaining focused on the breath. I recommend not taking notes. This might sound weird to some people. Yet listening this way allows us to have an astonishing experience. We create an inner space that completely absorbs what we are listening to without the urge to analyze and examine. There is a lot of room in this space for different opinions and perspectives. We are able to listen to people with different mind-sets and opinions without emotional reactions and judgments. We can allow things simply to be without arguing over them. Our relationships with customers and coworkers will change if we begin to listen to one another in this manner.

The power and the depth of our listening significantly determines what we are able to experience and learn. The quality of our listening even influences what can be said and what can't. When the speaker notices that no one is listening, he or she usually doesn't say much of significance. But when someone addresses attentive listeners, they speak in a more significant, respectful, and kinder way. It is important to persistently mitigate situations of inattentive listening or listening with negative energy. It is nothing but a waste of time and energy and causes frustration and separation.

I encourage you to evaluate the quality and feeling of your meetings and conversations. As we deepen our own listening, over time we will encounter opportunities to introduce ways of pausing, mindful breathing, and deep listening into our work routine.

The Smile as Our Default Response to Life

We have already mentioned the power of joy. And we know that every task feels easier to do with a smile on our face. It doesn't help to move through the day with a grouchy face. No matter how meaningful our work feels to us, without a smile, it will be harder. People don't smile enough in all their daily economic transactions. So it is up to us to create an economy whose actors' default response to life is a smile. Smiles improve with practice. We can invite a smile onto our face. And as we invite a conscious smile into our work, it can undergo a transformation.

A friend of mine teaches laughter yoga. As she guides them through simple exercises, participants are usually laughing heartily after a few minutes. A relaxed smile lightens our face and its energy radiates throughout our whole body. Let's gift ourselves and others with a smile! A smile invites us to laugh about ourselves and not take ourselves too seriously. With a smile, we can acknowledge our mistakes. A smile lets us connect with our difficult emotions so we can acknowledge them and take care of them. As soon as we smile in this way, we transform our work and our relationships. We suffuse work with a smile and share this gift with coworkers, customers, supervisors, and everyone else we encounter during the day.

Changing Our Work Attitude: Using the Four Levers of Transformation

Mindful breathing, work meditation, walking meditation, deep listening, smiling and practicing with mindfulness bells all allow us to cultivate mindfulness in different ways. As our mindfulness and presence increase with this practice, we will see more clearly how we feel, think, and perceive what is happening in our environment. This clarity rewards us with a lever to change our minds with patience and determination. Mindfulness is the prerequisite to apply the four levers of transformation (see illustration 6) or methods of right effort. These levers allow us to patiently transform the fragrance of our mind.

	Quality of the Seed	
	wholesome	unwholesome
mind consciousness (manifest)	holding **giving energy** offering space	acknowledge **embrace** don't engage
store consciousness (not yet manifest)	seek contact **invite** consciously touch	don't invite **protect** avoid contact

Seed Location

Illustration 6: Four levers for consciousness transformation

All of our mind's formations can be found in our store consciousness in the form of seeds or potentials. These are either wholesome or unwholesome formations; they may either lie dormant (not yet manifest) or are active (manifest). Together they result in four levers for the transformation of consciousness:

Invite. We invite dormant wholesome seeds to manifest. We can do this when we notice that we are inattentive. Or we might notice that we are angry with ourselves. We can practice loving kindness meditation and ask for the opposite ("May I be happy, and free of anger and discontent!"). By actively addressing the wholesome seeds within, we nourish our consciousness with wholesome food. By touching joy, we allow ourselves to become joy. Thich Nhat Hanh teaches: "There is no way to happiness; happiness is the way."

Giving energy. We feel joy. A wholesome seed made its way to the surface and blossoms. Now it is up to us to make time and space for joy in our consciousness. It is better to allow joy to spread for a while instead of having it replaced by the next impulse. We might have received an email from an old friend who appreciates our long friendship. Let's take the time to stay with the feeling of connectedness and unity. Let's refrain from opening the next email right away, which might be about an angry customer complaint. There is no need to run past the beauty in life. When we appreciate mind formations in this way, they are stronger on their next return into our store consciousness. It will be easier to activate them in the future.

Protect. We take caution to neither encourage nor provoke the rise of unwholesome seeds. We become aware of the triggers that increase our anger and unhappiness. We avoid and reduce contact with people, situations, media, or environments that may activate unwholesome seeds. We become aware of the things that are harmful to our consciousness and those that poison it. We learn to protect ourselves using intelligent methods.

Embrace. When negative seeds arise, we don't give them additional energy. We don't engage emotionally, but follow our breath mindfully. We don't add fuel to the fire. We neither lose our temper nor do we let our discontent escalate. We simply acknowledge what is happening mindfully. Our unwholesome mind formation loses energy when we embrace it in that way, and the unwholesome seed returns weakened into the store consciousness.

As we use these four levers every day, we become active gardeners of our consciousness. We strengthen the wholesome and weaken the unwholesome.

Paying Attention to Every Step

As our mindfulness deepens, we understand the importance of every small step more clearly. So many of the steps we take every day seem inconspicuous or insignificant. We write routine emails, drink coffee, make phone calls, attend meetings, go to the restroom, say hello to colleagues, meet clients, take breaks, eat lunch, and work on presentations. Paying attention to every step implies that we perform every single one of these activities mindfully, that we acknowledge their significance, impact, and meaning. No action is insignificant. A friendly hello in the hallway influences the next meeting.

Economic thinking often focuses on the future. We work on strategies, develop plans and goals, define milestones and career goals. The current small step, and the current day seem insignificant next to the important goals in the future. We learn to sacrifice the present for the benefit of the future. This maxim is equally woven into our education system (future diplomas), stock exchanges (future returns), and politics (future elections). Our thoughts are so focused on the future that we may miss the present. But if we lose our presence in the midst of our activities, we deprive our actions of clarity, effectiveness, and compassion. A manager shared the following in a discussion group:

First I studied for my high school diploma, then for my college degrees and my dissertation. There was always another summit

to climb. This did not end during my professional life. When my
wife asked for a divorce, I had no clue why she did it. It was
a heart attack that finally brought me to my senses. I realized
that I had rushed by the important things all of my life. I had chil-
dren, but I never spent time with them. Even when we played, my
thoughts stayed with my work projects. Now I learn to focus on my
current step and it feels like entering a new life. How could I have
been so blind?

Something is wrong if a future goal leads to our being unhappy, stressed, or angry over long stretches of time. Our life can wither in the shade of an important goal.

Thich Nhat Hanh always emphasizes: "The best way to take care of the future is to take good care of the present moment." By paying attention to the present moment, we take good care of the future. It is hard to wrap one's mind around this. If it was easy, we wouldn't plan, worry, expect, or speculate so much. Mark Twain expressed this sentiment similarly: "The worst things in my life never happened." If we stay with what is, we are on the safe side. Then we can engage with the reality we face in this moment.

Plans can provide helpful guidelines, but they shouldn't distract us from the living reality of the current steps. Too many deadlines will stunt our creativity. If we are primarily focused on the outcome, we run the risk of losing sight of the steps toward the goal. Therefore, the likelihood that we may stray from the path increases. We might take shortcuts to get what we want. There is no end that justifies unwholesome means. There would have been no financial crisis in 2008 if all economical players had paid attention to the quality of their steps instead of falling prey to the promises of a distant future.

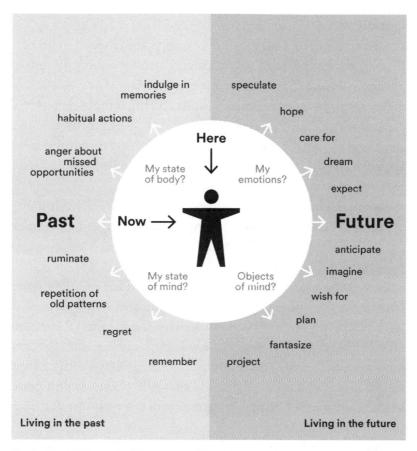

Illustration 7: The pull of the past and the future

If we pay attention to our present step, we can clearly feel: "Oh, this step makes me feel uncomfortable," or "This doesn't feel right." These are alarm signals, safeguards, stop signals that protect us from future accidents. We can easily miss them if we keep staring rigidly into the future.

The past can also pull us away from the present. We ruminate, mourn, indulge in memories, and regret missed opportunities. That is the pull of the past. Speculation, worries, and fantasies are the pull of the future. Our mental energy is not unlimited—we have to use it wisely.

Realistic Visions

On the fifth day of a mindfulness seminar for entrepreneurs, the CEO of a large company asked Thich Nhat Hanh how he should advise his managers on the upcoming Monday.

"How can you manage mindfulness and implement it in a large organization?" was the basis of his question. Thich Nhat Hanh recommended that he begin patiently cultivating mindfulness on his own: "Begin to change yourself, practice mindfulness, and walk patiently step for step."

Practicing in this way, we will recognize when we are ready to share insights with others and implement changes in the work structure, because we have experienced them within ourselves and in our practice.

Companies where employees engage in mindfulness are superior in many ways to those that don't employ this concept. They can act more effectively, and they will focus energy on the most important tasks instead of wasting energy by engaging in unnecessary conflicts, power games, or wrong perceptions. The change starts with us. How can we ask our potential cofighters to change if we can't or don't want to change? Change begins with us and with our next mindful step.

Practice, Don't Fantasize

Mindfulness is neither an intellectual idea nor a theoretical ideal, but rather a mental ability that requires daily practice. Many visionary and utopian communities failed because they couldn't live out their ideals in their day-to-day life. A commitment to love is simply not enough to be capable of love or to become a loving person. If we want to love, we need to learn how to act and think in a loving way and to practice and develop the spirit of love in our day-to-day life. This isn't easy. It requires daily practice.

There is no way that we can create true peace as long as we are holding anger, irritation, and grudges against ourselves and others. We won't be able to make the case for greater material justice while we are still dominated by unfulfilled wishes and unhappiness. It is important to keep practicing our transformation patiently, resolutely, and with courage.

Patience is important to master the personal process of transformation with all its successes and failures. We will mature gradually.

Courage is crucial because we have to accept personal responsibility to make changes. We might have to leave a comfortable, well-paid position that harms us mentally. We might have to try something new.

Determination is crucial, because we need to look at our bad work habits and the central activities in our lives with a beginner's mind, ready to make changes.

It helps to get together with like-minded people and start organizations where people work together more joyfully, freely, and consciously in meaningful ways. As we embody mindfulness, the fundamental coordinates of our work life change. Karl Riedl, director of the Interbeing Center, says:

> Over the years our meditation center grew and had as many overnight guests as a midsize hotel. We record the highest number of overnight stays in the county of Freyung-Grafenau {in Bavaria, Germany}. Every task in our house is performed as work meditation—we call it joyful doing. One time, a man who was very familiar with the hotel business stayed with us. He observed our daily routines very carefully and was increasingly surprised over the course of his stay. After a while he asked us: "How are you doing it? How do you organize everything? A regular business of this size would require so many staff. Yet everything seems to run so easily and seems almost self-organized here." I answered him: "When every single task is performed with mindfulness, it makes all the difference in the world."

The True Nature of Work

What kind of work do I do? What tasks do I perform? Which choices do I make, consciously or unconsciously? What are the effects of these choices? What kind of impact does my work environment have on me?

Work is much more than a way to fulfill our material needs. Our work provides us with the opportunity to grow, to serve, and to contribute. When we make full use of the potential of our work, we gain a greater understanding of ourselves and of the world.

In Zen, work is perceived as a path. We recognize ourselves in our work. We always make an active contribution to every kind of work, whether we are artists, craftsmen, entrepreneurs, or run-of-the-mill employees. It can be a lifelong process to truly understand the work we do, to permeate it, to become one with it and achieve true mastery of it. If we work in this way, we will encounter all of the obstacles of life: our different moods, changes in our work environment, all the different ingredients of life that continuously reassemble in new ways and continually surprise us with different outcomes. As soon as the process of work becomes mechanical, our growth is stunted. Life is not a repetition. It is a fresh start every day. Mastery can grow from an open mind and a work ethic like that. If we master our work in this way, we will better master our life as well.

Some people see work as a mere job or a necessary evil. Some see work as a means to climb up the career ladder and appear successful. Work can serve as a status symbol or a sign of affiliation to a certain group. The amazing potential that work offers us isn't realized in so many work lives. Mindfulness can help us to answer the following questions:

- What is it that makes us sick in our work life?
  What benefits our physical and mental health?

- How can we break free of limiting and restricting jobs? How do we find new meaning?

- How can we find true joy in our work and get in contact with positive energy?

- How do we find work that aligns with our ethical values?

- How do we let go of the judgments of others and develop a realistic, positive standard for our actions?

- How can we align our financial demands and our wish for meaningful work?

- How will we find an environment that supports our wholesome sides and advances our talents?

- How do we find the right balance between not being challenged enough and having excessive demands and stress?

Not a single position or work situation is identical with another. While we may be able to influence some areas with our inner disposition and training of our mind, others present us with organizational, systemic, or societal obstacles and myths. Mindfulness helps us to differentiate what we can change and influence, where we may find a compromise, and when we need to protect ourselves from destructive forces. We are capable of a lot as individuals, but we also shouldn't overestimate our powers.

First we will look at certain myths prevalent in the work world, and then we will present central possibilities that allow us to make choices in the field of work.

Myths and Distortions of Work
How are our hopes, expectations, and fears in the field of work

created? How do our concepts of normal, good, or bad work develop? Many young people have difficulties forming a realistic mental concept of working life. Our impressions of work are strongly influenced by our parents' work realities and our close surroundings. We fall into a practical and emotional work legacy. We lack personal experiences, and so we struggle to arrive at a realistic assessment.

The following influences also contribute:

- Lack of transparency from the outside about the true nature of a profession, an industry, an employer, or a specific position

- Buying into the beliefs of peer groups: friends, acquaintances, other students

- Lack of or limited number of positions in the region people live in

- Unrealistic representation of professions in the media

- High competition for dream jobs and fashionable professions

- Little reported experience in new professions and fields of work

All these factors make us vulnerable to myths and prejudices. As a young man, I was quite naive when I started my professional training. After I arrived in my fancy blue suit, I was sent into a stuffy room where I stamped and folded advertising pamphlets for days on end. I experienced the infamous reality shock. Some illusions clear up quickly. Others stay with us all our lives. It is worth examining these illusions.

Myth: Dirty and Menial Work Should Be Avoided
We tend to hold certain types of work in high regard and look down

on others. These hierarchies differ from society to society, but they always cause division and tension in the individual and the collective. They need to be broken up.

In some Zen monasteries, the abbot regularly cleans the toilets. This practice reminds the monastery leaders to stay humble and do any meaningful work indiscriminately. We let go of the idea that there is inferior work we need to avoid and superior work we want to strive for.

We connect with the dignity, and the intrinsic value of work. It is both useful and necessary to clean toilets. Let me share a story that the president of a Japanese company shared:

> A while ago we had trouble with graffiti. It occurred time and time again in our restrooms. We admonished, threatened, repainted, but whatever we tried, there was another incident. One day there was a note pinned to the wall that read: "Please don't dirty my good workplace with your smearing." It was the clumsy writing of our old cleaning woman. I wasn't the only one touched by this message. After that, there was no more graffiti on the walls; not a single instance. We were all very impressed.[3]

Myth: Work Is Hard and Painstaking

Close your eyes and say the word *work* quietly to yourself. How does the word *work* sound to you? What are the connotations and feelings that come up? We all have different work biographies, but our culture is deeply characterized by a Protestant work ethic. "Success is based on hard work. Work is serious." Rolex runs an ad with this slogan: "Be hard to the wind and hard to yourself."

The word *work* is highly charged in our culture. Work isn't easy when the collective field around us operates with effort, seriousness, obligation, struggle, and competition. We should try to tap into other

---

3. Shunduo Aoyama: Pflaumenblüten im Schnee: Gedanken einer japanischen Zen-Meisterin (Bielefeld, Germany: Theseus, 1995), 75.

qualities of work during our workday: qualities like joy, relaxation, human connectedness, and even lightness.

Myth: Work and Personal Life Should Be Separated

Many people separate their private and professional lives and distinguish between work and non-work. "This is private; it is no one's business," they might say. Or: "Business before pleasure." Oftentimes this attitude is supposed to act as a safeguard from the demands of professional life. We want to shield our private world from professional impositions and standards. We don't want any professional rules to interfere with our private life. We also don't want to impact our reputation or career by our private behavior. Unless we are careful, we will develop a double life in this way. What is allowed professionally isn't permitted privately. What we allow ourselves privately is taboo professionally. Private life or professional life may become a comfort zone, where we recover from the demands of the other state of being.

This separation between work and non-work can have a number of consequences. This division may unconsciously affect all different kinds of our activities. We might use a different voice and different emotions on the phone talking to our clients as opposed to a handyman who works for us privately. We walk differently through the hallway in our office than when we walk toward the supermarket. The separation happens in our head. Of course there are some activities that we exclusively perform in our jobs. But the majority of our private and professional tasks are essentially identical: breathing, walking, eating, dealing with emotions, speaking, listening. There is no separate work world apart from our regular being. The following equation expresses the connection:

being > activity > work > gainful employment

The more we create a mental separation between our work and

the rest of our lives, the more tension arises. The more we let our professional role, expectations, and self-images rule us, the more disruptions we create in the other parts of our lives. The idea that we can separate the private and the professional is an illusion. The private always penetrates the professional, and our professional life permeates and colors the private, no matter how much we want to protect them from one another. If we can find work that allows us to be ourselves and where there is no need to pretend otherwise, we can avoid these dilemmas.

Myth: We Need to Find a Job We Love

Do you feel the longing for a job that is tailor-made for you? Do you have the feeling that this job must exist somewhere out there? A job that will need our talents, our values, our wishes? We feel that our being special and unique requires work that is special and unique. Here we need to be careful to avoid the pitfall of individualization. We are prone to falsely believe that the perfect kind of work will rescue us from an unpleasant situation.

Love is quite similar. We might hope to meet the one and only person destined to be our soul mate. This attitude will cause problems whether it is in love or work. We are looking outward rather than inward. We aren't quite as special as we like to think. Instead of spending a lot of our energy and thoughts about some special position perfectly tailored to our desires, we might choose to walk a different path. We can learn how to love. A friend of mine, the Buddhist abbess Sister Jina, said: "If you can't do what you love, you need to learn to love what you do."

Let me share the experience of a practitioner in work meditation:

I raked leaves in the garden with two other people. We worked in silence and kept a steady pace. There was so much joy, and it felt harmonious! I realized how much I missed harmonious community in my day-to-day working life. I had always assumed that I needed challenging work assignments to be happy. Now I stood here, raking, and I was happy.

Our search for the perfect solution can be the cause for numerous frustrations. Our culture emphasizes the individual. We focus on what separates us instead of what unites us. If we cling to the idea of a dream job, we might lose our way and be disappointed in the short and long-term.

Myth: Jobs are Necessary, No Matter What

We hear from our politicians almost daily that the need to create and retain jobs is of the highest priority. Whoever creates jobs, either by winning over companies to build a headquarters in a particular town or by saving jobs that are "threatened," is celebrated as a hero. The German president Horst Köhler once said: "We need to do whatever we can to create new jobs. Initiatives that serve other goals are subordinate, no matter how desirable they may be."

Is it presumptuous to question this statement?

There exists a big individual and collective fear of a world without work, a world in which we are running out of jobs. The government is afraid of reduced tax revenues and social instability, individuals fear unemployment and losing their financial existence, trade unions worry about losing their members. Therefore, work above all!

This way of thinking leads to the creation and perpetuation of a society that will employ the highest number of people possible. Instead of producing what we truly need, and working an appropriate amount to do so, we need to make more and more efforts to utilize existing and future production capacities. Rather than being able to enjoy more free time to spend with our families and the extra space for personal development that new technologies might provide for us, our desires keep growing.

We need to realize that the basis for mental well-being in a society isn't having as many people as possible gainfully employed, but rather when as many people as possible do meaningful work. Social entrepreneurship organizations disrupt "work above all" thinking by insisting on meaningful and wholesome causes as main motivators instead of market opportunities. We don't need just any type of work. We need work that is meaningful to society.

Choice in Our Work: Do We Have a Choice, or Are Decisions Imposed on Us?

Not too many of us are able to choose where we work. At first glance, many parts of the population are limited to a very small number of job opportunities due to geographical limitations, education, and immediate financial obligations. Some have no options at all. There are real barriers to choice. But we discover, as we look more deeply, that an enormous potential of creativity is lost in the field of work due to fearful, unconscious, and narrow-minded decisions. We remain stuck in careers and meaningless jobs instead of making other choices. I have personal experience with this:

> *Zürich, October 1997. I have reached the end of my academic education. In four short months I will finish my dissertation on "Knowledge Management" at the University of Geneva. I am fortunate enough to have choices. I received an offer from Holderbank, an international cement company. I am confused and not sure what I want to do. Finally, I decide to follow the path that last years' students chose. I apply at the most esteemed management consultant organizations. A few weeks later, after an exhausting interview process, I sign a contract with McKinsey & Company. I didn't really decide. The decision was made for me.*

It Is Up to Us to Choose, and We Do Have a Choice

Many people equate freedom with the ability to have many options and to keep these options open as long as possible. When I ask business students about their future career goals, most of them answer: "I want to keep as many options open as possible." This approach doesn't seem very helpful, in my opinion. Freedom, for me, means being able to make decisions mindfully and consciously. Freedom means closing doors, excluding certain options for good reasons instead of trying to keep all options open perpetually. In the long run, of course, it is impossible to keep your options open forever. Making free choices in life gives humans dignity. We make decisions because we believe in something. We choose a life partner, a family, a teacher, a community, a profession, and a lifestyle.

Many people see themselves as victims in the workforce. They feel unfree, they don't believe they have any options. They perform their work without joy and deem it pointless. They perceive themselves as victims of entrepreneurs, of the markets, of their supervisors, of colleagues, or of the whole society. While certain things are out of our control, we need to take responsibility for what we can. While at Plum Village, a prospective monk told me:

> *During my first three years in the monastery, my mind kept complaining about this and that. If I had one thing, I wanted another. If I had this, I wanted that. My mentor kept telling me: "Stop the complaining mind." Make a decision and live with its consequences. Take responsibility for your decisions and live with their consequences.*

If we play the role of the victim and avoid decisions, we are wasting our energy. Our current situation is the result of many conscious and unconscious choices in our life.

Now I will introduce six dimensions of choice in our work.

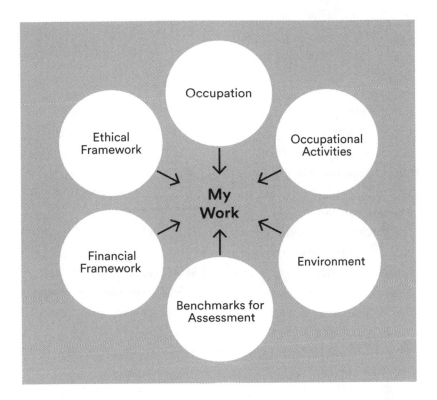

Illustration 8: Central dimensions of choice in our work

Selecting an Ethical Framework

Do we clearly understand which ethical principles guide us? Do we make basic ethical decisions? Do we take the time to practice our framework?

Many leading economists have long insisted that the economy isn't responsible for answers to ethical questions. An economy without any ethical foundation, however, can dramatically harm society. We learned this during the financial crisis of 2008 and 2009. A banker I worked with said the following:

> *We barely escaped the meltdown of the whole world economy. Now we need a lot more than stronger regulations of the markets. We won't master this crisis on an intellectual basis alone; we do need*

> *ethical change, I would say, deep ethical insights that will touch*
> *our hearts and change not only our economic activities, but our*
> *thinking about the economy.*

It is not just "the economy" that is in need of a clear ethical grounding. Every human being is enacting ethics in their lives in some way, whether they are aware of it or not. It is our task to become aware and consciously choose our ethical grounding. This decision has far-reaching effects on our work. We need a kind of ethics that helps us to stay the course in our work.

Ethics is a vast field. We can distinguish between intentional ethics and applied ethics. Intentional ethics is based on a catalog of commandments and prohibitions that we accept internally and try to abide by. Applied ethics is based on similar concepts, but expects that we primarily use our own experiences to verify the validity of its ethical precepts. In intentional ethics, we might be told that lies are a sin. In applied ethics, we see for ourselves that lies have many negative impacts in our lives, and try to avoid them.

Mindfulness helps us to gain this direct insight into the impacts of our actions. Mindfulness meditation gives us direct insight into the ethical dimension of our actions. In the presence of mindfulness, we recognize the effects our actions have upon ourselves and others. A small lie will cause immediate tension in our body, restlessness in our mind, and a residual feeling of fear. We also feel a sense of joy, trust, equanimity, and peace when we communicate honestly. This experience deepens our trust in the ethical guideline of striving for truthfulness. We understand that unethical behavior, in our work and elsewhere, not only harms others but also ourselves.

This lucid experience provides us with insights that lend a clear direction to our work and life. As our mindfulness deepens, it becomes more and more natural for us to avoid activities that harm ourselves and others.

The Five Mindfulness Trainings, developed by Thich Nhat Hanh and rooted in the Five Precepts taught by the Buddha, are my ethical framework. Many parts of the Mindfulness Trainings are largely in agreement with other religious, spiritual, and philosophical ethical systems. What I find unique, however, is the emphasis on mindfulness. Without mindfulness there cannot be any depth to our ethics. How can I act ethically if I am not fully aware of what I am doing? In the following I will introduce the Five Mindfulness Trainings, and you can see whether they are helpful for you.

The First Mindfulness Training: Reverence for Life

Aware of the suffering caused by the destruction of life, I am committed to cultivating the insight of interbeing and compassion and learning ways to protect the lives of people, animals, plants, and minerals. I am determined not to kill, not to let others kill, and not to support any act of killing in the world, in my thinking, or in my way of life. Seeing that harmful actions arise from anger, fear, greed, and intolerance, which in turn come from dualistic and discriminative thinking, I will cultivate openness, nondiscrimination, and nonattachment to views in order to transform violence, fanaticism, and dogmatism in myself and in the world.

The Second Mindfulness Training: True Happiness

Aware of the suffering caused by exploitation, social injustice, stealing, and oppression, I am committed to practicing generosity in my thinking, speaking, and acting. I am determined not to steal and not to possess anything that should belong to others; and I will share my time, energy, and material resources with those who are in need. I will practice looking deeply to see that the happiness and suffering of others are not separate from my own happiness and suffering; that true happiness is not possible without understanding and compassion; and that running after wealth, fame, power, and sensual pleasures can bring much suffering and despair. I am aware that happiness depends on my mental attitude and not on external conditions, and that I can live happily in the present moment simply by remembering that I already have more than enough conditions to be happy. I am committed to practicing Right Livelihood so that I can help reduce the suffering of living beings on earth and stop contributing to climate change.

The Third Mindfulness Training: True Love

Aware of the suffering caused by sexual misconduct, I am committed to cultivating responsibility and learning ways to protect the safety and integrity of individuals, couples, families, and society. Knowing that sexual desire is not love, and that sexual activity motivated by craving always harms myself as well as others, I am determined not to engage in sexual relations without true love and a deep, long-term commitment made known to my family and friends. I will do everything in my power to protect children from sexual abuse and to prevent couples and families from being broken by sexual misconduct. Seeing that body and mind are one, I am committed to learning appropriate ways to take care of my sexual energy and cultivating loving kindness, compassion, joy, and inclusiveness—which are the four basic elements of true love—for my greater happiness and the greater happiness of others. Practicing true love, we know that we will continue beautifully into the future.

The Fourth Mindfulness Training: Loving Speech and Deep Listening

Aware of the suffering caused by unmindful speech and the inability to listen to others, I am committed to cultivating loving speech and compassionate listening in order to relieve suffering and to promote reconciliation and peace in myself and among other people, ethnic and religious groups, and nations. Knowing that words can create happiness or suffering, I am committed to speaking truthfully using words that inspire confidence, joy, and hope. When anger is manifesting in me, I am determined not to speak. I will practice mindful breathing and walking in order to recognize and to look deeply into my anger. I know that the roots of anger can be found in my wrong perceptions and lack of understanding of the suffering in myself and in the other person. I will speak and listen in a way that can help myself and the other person to transform suffering and see the way out of difficult situations. I am determined not to spread news that I do not know to be certain and not to utter words that can cause division or discord. I will practice Right Diligence to nourish my capacity for understanding, love, joy, and inclusiveness, and gradually transform anger, violence, and fear that lie deep in my consciousness.

The Fifth Mindfulness Training: Nourishment and Healing

Aware of the suffering caused by unmindful consumption, I am committed to cultivating good health, both physical and mental, for myself, my family, and my society by practicing mindful eating, drinking, and consuming. I will practice looking deeply into how I consume the Four Kinds of Nutriments, namely edible foods, sense impressions, volition, and consciousness. I am determined not to gamble, or to use alcohol, drugs, or any other products that contain toxins, such as certain websites, electronic games, TV programs, films, magazines, books, and conversations. I will practice coming back to the present moment to be in touch with the refreshing, healing, and nourishing elements in me and around me, not letting regrets and sorrow drag me back into the past nor letting anxieties, fear, or craving pull me out of the present moment. I am determined not to try to cover up loneliness, anxiety, or other suffering by losing myself in consumption. I will contemplate interbeing and consume in a way that preserves peace, joy, and well-being in my body and consciousness, and in the collective body and consciousness of my family, my society, and the earth.

These statements are not absolute rules. They offer a path of practice we consciously choose. No one is able to observe the mindfulness trainings perfectly. They give us a direction, show us the way, and humble us.

When we accept the orientation provided by the mindfulness trainings for our work, they give us a lens through which to observe our work environment. Organizations, just like people, aren't perfect. We won't find a real life example of a perfect company. It makes a huge difference if we are able to choose a work environment where the orientation of the mindfulness trainings is respected or even one which abides by an honest mission statement. However, if we work in a place where we encounter constant ridicule, contempt, and hostility toward these or other ethical values, it will be very difficult for us to live our truth.

How to Choose a Profession

What is the right livelihood for me? Why do I work in this field or profession? Who pays me? What is the fragrance of this income?

Our livelihood requires money. In Buddhism we speak of the ideal of "right livelihood." This refers to work that aligns with our values and supports rather than harms our mental development.

Every field of work, every profession, and every organization has its own culture and a number of explicit and implicit values and convictions. We choose to abide by these standards to a certain degree when we enter a professional field.

There is no need to hastily condemn whole industries, companies, and professions. Yet there are certain professions that make it particularly hard to live in agreement with the mindfulness trainings. Thich Nhat Hanh writes:

> *Our vocations can nourish our understanding and compassion, or erode them.... A job that includes killing, stealing, sexual misconduct, lying, or selling drugs or alcohol is not Right Livelihood.*[4]

Buddha advised his students to avoid certain professions. We protect ourselves by excluding certain professions, industries, and

---

4. Thich Nhat Hanh, *The Heart of the Buddha's Teaching* (New York: Harmony Books, 1998).

companies as fields of work. We make sure that our work is in line with our ethical principles. This is right livelihood. We are aware that many sectors of modern industry are harmful to humans and to nature, so we don't participate in these processes.

The way people make their living influences all other human beings. Therefore, right livelihood is a collective matter. We make an effort to find work that benefits humans, animals, plants, and the earth, in which the harm caused by our work is minimal. Thich Nhat Hanh takes this even further:

> *The way you support yourself can be an expression of your deepest self, or it can be a source of suffering for you and others. ... If you are able to work in a profession that helps realize your ideal of compassion, be grateful. And please try to help create proper jobs for others by living mindfully, simply, and sanely. ... If someone has a profession that causes living beings to suffer and oppresses others, it will infect their own consciousness, just as when we pollute the air that we ourselves have to breathe.[5]*

As we are able to become more mindful, we can see the impact of our actions more clearly. It gives us pleasure when we develop and sell a useful product. We become aware of guilt and shame when we persuade someone to buy a product that we would never consider to purchase. When we are in direct contact with the results of our own work, it is much easier to make a change and stay the course. Our life and our work will develop in a more relaxed and stable direction when we align our actions with the Five Mindfulness Trainings.

Choosing Meaningful Occupations

Is my occupation meaningful? What are the goals and ideals I dedicate my energy to?

When we talk about work, we are usually referring to gainful

---

5. Ibid.

employment: labor for money. And we assume that there is a corresponding relationship between how useful a particular kind of work is and what the payment is. That isn't always the case, however. What kind of immaterial and monetary values are assigned to occupations is a collective choice that we make.

Gainful employment is not necessarily meaningful. Unpaid work can be indispensable. This distinction is very helpful for me to assess my daily activities. I can ask myself every night whether the work I performed that day was meaningful or not. The line between paid and unpaid work begins to blur and all activities can be examined with respect to their usefulness. We know that we are on the right track when our activities at the office, and with our family, neighbors, and friends become more meaningful and head toward a healthy direction.

When we pursue questions of meaning, it is dangerous to rely on feedback from the world of work. We can make more and more money while we perform meaningless tasks. High-paying work can destroy our society.

Meaningful activities advance us personally and as a society. The kind deeds of mothers and fathers, sons and daughters, and countless volunteers hold our society together. Creating a more mindful economy requires reconnecting gainful employment with its actual meaning.

We should ask ourselves why some of the most meaningful social work is also some of the most poorly paid work, or incompletely paid, or not paid at all, while some of the most pointless activities are paid exorbitantly well. Good work is not necessarily paid well. This is only a small comfort for those who keep struggling financially despite doing excellent and useful work.

Initiatives that support a universal basic income trust in people's desire for meaningful work. Those favoring a basic income don't assume that recipients are simply lazy, but that they would like to realize their dream of useful employment and hope to break free from pointless work conditions.

University of St. Gallen, Switzerland, May 1995. This is a golden moment in my college years. I am listening to an entrepreneur whom I had never heard of. He has been invited to the St. Gallen Symposium (ISC) and talks in simple English about his unorthodox initiatives fighting poverty in his homeland of Bangladesh. The whole audience is captivated. This is someone who has wholeheartedly dedicated himself to a meaningful cause and speaks with joy, clarity, honesty and love about his work, and his colleagues. We are listening to Mohammed Yunus. Eleven years later, he wins the Nobel Peace Prize together with Grameen Bank/Bank for the Poor, which he founded.

All of us who listened to that speech were deeply impressed. Yunus touched us deeply, yet we all still followed our prescribed career paths. We didn't have the courage to attempt to become intimate with the question of meaning in our work lives.

November 2008. The seeds planted by Muhammad Yunus have borne fruit. I participate in the Vision Summit, a conference in Berlin where {Yunus's} ideas are introduced and discussed under the heading of "Social Entrepreneurship." The spirit of optimism is palpable among the 1,000 participants in the halls of the Henry Ford Building at the Free University of Berlin.

It is a wonderful experience to witness people tear down the walls of their self-constructed work prison when they realize that they are freer than they thought and turn toward more meaningful activities. More and more people seem to be ready to leave relatively secure and highly paid positions because they are looking for something more. Each one of us has the opportunity for self-inquiry and redirection. A participant at the Vision Summit said:

Two years ago I finished my MBA at an elite university. Consultants and investment bankers presented positions to my class, and almost everyone ended up in their "dream job." The reality, however, is anything but a dream. More than half of my fellow students no longer enjoy their work, nor do they find it meaningful. I am feeling the same way.

More and more talented people are looking for meaning and are ready to leave the comforts and financial safety net of the mainstream workforce.

Choosing a Meaningful Environment

Who is allowed to shape and mold us? To whom do we give our energy?

We easily underestimate the influence of our environment. Humans are permeable beings in constant contact with their surroundings. We continue manifesting in new ways. As we are in constant contact with our peers, we adopt elements of them over time, whether consciously or unconsciously. They "interpenetrate" us. Many who arrived before us leave their imprint on us. Our own effective force is quite limited. We might feel differently from our colleagues, but we can't help but absorb the dominant essence of our environment. We are not separate from our environment. We can't move in our environment and avoid being influenced by it.

What does this mean for our work?

Aware of the significant influence of our work environment on us, we shouldn't choose our jobs or our career lightly. We are relatively free in our society to choose our initial environment. After we enter it, however, it shapes us, and then we lose a part of our freedom. During work retreats, employees always discuss how hard it is to maintain mindfulness in an unmindful environment. When we are tired or having a bad day, we literally feel how negativity creeps into our consciousness.

I have also witnessed the opposite. When I visit Plum Village, my spiritual home, upon entering the monastery site and in my first encounters with monks, nuns, and practitioners, I notice how I am filled with the energy of concentration and mindfulness. I immerse myself in this environment and consciously take it all in. It is a wonderful experience to be touched by these wholesome mental formations. After a short while I emerge in a more peaceful, clearer, and happier mental state. It is truly remarkable. We are our environment.

Anyone who has experienced the benefits of working and living in a mindful environment will gain new insights regarding their own work environment. What we accepted as normal in the past won't seem normal anymore at all. We experienced a new way of working together. And we don't want to limit this experience to the time we spend in a mindfulness center; we want to also utilize it in our daily work. The contrast between the atmosphere in a mindfulness center and our own work reality can trigger a crisis. Here are some testimonies:

> When I returned to work after a two-week visit at Plum Village, I became aware of the vibes between coworkers and was able to observe how conflicts arose. First there were only remarks and gestures, which after a while escalated into a fight.

> Working together in mindfulness showed me what my job was missing. There is no space for listening or simply stopping to smile. Our daily routine is overly hectic. I don't want to work this way anymore. I am looking for others who want to work together in a mindful way.

Visiting a mindfulness center is very helpful if we want to better understand the energy of mindfulness. It is also an opportunity to examine the ideas introduced in this book firsthand. Personal and direct experience are invaluable. Work meditation can reward us with insights that can revolutionize our work life. This is a lesson that everyone needs to experience firsthand, on their own.

Consciously choosing a nourishing environment is not the same as retreating from a difficult area of society into a comfort zone. It only means that we create a setting where our wholesome seeds, attitudes, and talents can receive enough sustenance to grow stronger. We will then be able to return into difficult fields and be more effective, as our practice is strong and we are internally stable.

Choosing a Standard for Evaluation

Who evaluates me? Whose evaluation is important to me? Do I have the criteria to evaluate myself?

Our work experience depends to a great degree on our own standards of judgment. One person might perceive a certain job as a symbol of personal failure, while another might thrive in the very same position and see it as a dream job. We all have internal and external standards for evaluation.

Internal standards refer to the expectations we have for ourselves, our ambitions, and the self-perception of our accomplishments. These standards also depend on the intensity and strength of our own inner critic.

Exterior standards of evaluation in the work field are formal performance evaluations, reports, praise and criticism, salary increases and cuts, layoffs, promotions, and feedback of any kind from the outside world.

Human beings can be judged before they are even born: "A girl? How wonderful!" And after we enter the world, parents, neighbors, kindergarten teachers, teachers, trainers, professors, and many more judge us according to their standards. Our family of origin, the social class we were raised in, our friends, and society as a whole have standards. We can accept, ignore, or reject these notions, but we will be impacted by them regardless. We either conform or rebel. We cannot help being shaped by standards, but we can also choose how to shape ourselves.

How freely we can move within the field of praise and criticism depends mainly on our own awareness. When we practice mindfulness, we can see more accurately which standards we use to judge ourselves and others.

When we choose our own evaluation standards, we begin to:

- develop our own evaluation standards for our work

- become less attached to complying with mainstream society

- become less attached to praise and less reactive to criticism

- separate ourselves from our inner critic

- recognize manipulations and not fall for them

- become less prone to emotional entanglements

We are often our own harshest critics. We can be highly unforgiving and unkind. When we are aware of the internal and external standards we're using, we put distance between ourselves and our judgments and may be able to choose inspiring role models and mentors.

Choosing a Financial Framework

How much money do I need? What is the right lifestyle for me?

There is an old American worker song with the chorus: "I owe, I owe, so off to work I go." Financial dependencies and obligations function to keep us locked into place and afraid to make changes in our lives. In seminars, I often meet the main breadwinners in the family who share how unhappy they are in their jobs, yet don't see any way possible to live beneath their current income. Financial fears may paralyze our courage to begin anew professionally.

It is helpful to review our monthly budget, our financial norms, and what we consider our financial "essentials." We might find that it is possible to live more simply and to make a change. It is not necessarily noble to make less money, however, and I am not advocating making blind or rash decisions. But if we need to make change in our work life, we should think calmly about what our true financial needs are.

The Interbeing of the Dimensions of Choice

When we examine our current work situation, we realize how decisions that have been made in the six areas of choice interact and influence each other. As soon as we choose a highly paid profession, we exclude lower paid—possibly more meaningful—professions and occupational fields. When we decide to favor a particular ethical framework, we exclude certain professions, occupations, and environments.

We might also be in the midst of a stage of life that comes with very little choice—whether that is because we are responsible for children, sick parents, or simply have a number of financial obligations. Yet our life is in constant flux. We inherit money and gain some financial freedom. Our children grow up and we engage in different activities. Our practice deepens and we see the beauty of a simple life. The dimensions of our work life change constantly. No one holds a lifelong job these days, as used to be customary. The more clearly we can visualize the choices presented in this chapter, the more freedom we gain to move around in our work life and engage in meaningful activities. We can always choose anew.

Proper Work-Life Balance

How much do I work? Is there a balance? Do I keep the right work-life balance?

Individuals, society, and humanity as a whole aren't particularly capable of moderating themselves. We overfish the oceans, we heat up the earth, and we pile up debt for future generations. The field of work is imbalanced in many areas. Millions of people are unemployed, while many others work more than they themselves or their families can bear. Chronic exhaustion, burnout, depression, and drug abuse in the workplace are on the rise. University graduates expect to work seventy-hour weeks at the beginning of their careers. Workaholics can be found everywhere, among physicians, investment bankers, music producers, politicians, and entrepreneurs. When the world is out of balance, we must hold up our own. Without the right balance, we are in danger of losing our physical and mental health.

The Middle Way

Buddhism teaches the Middle Way, the way that finds balance between extremes. A key story describes the encounter between Buddha and his student Sona, who had a difficult time finding the right balance for his meditation practice in his day-to-day life. He went through phases of great zeal followed by extreme exhaustion and frustration. The following dialogue between Buddha and Sona has been handed down in the Sona Sutra:

"Now what do you think, Sona. Before, when you were a housedweller, were you skilled at playing the vina?"

"Yes, lord."

"And what do you think: when the strings of your vina were too taut, was your vina in tune and playable?"

"No, lord."

"And what do you think: when the strings of your vina were too loose, was your vina in tune and playable?"

"No, lord."

"And what do you think: when the strings of your vina were neither too taut nor too loose, but tuned to be right on pitch, was your vina in tune and playable?"

"Yes, lord."

"In the same way, Sona, over-aroused persistence leads to restlessness, overly slack persistence leads to laziness. Thus you should determine the right pitch for your persistence, attune ('penetrate,' 'ferret out') the pitch of the [five] faculties [to that], and there pick up your theme."[6]

Examples of Excessiveness

During the industrial revolution, many men, women, and children worked themselves to death in mines, factories, and on construction sites. There is no question that they worked way too much. They were exploited, and their employers had lost all sense of how to relate to human beings. Humans are limited creatures with vulnerable bodies and fragile minds. Without a certain balance, we harm ourselves. We need protection against exploitation.

In the Western world we are protected today by extensive labor laws. Weekly working hours are limited in many areas. Participation rights and labor laws protect us against excessive exploitation. This is remarkable progress. Exploitation, of course, continues to exist. In many areas we simply exported the problem to countries with poorer labor protection. This is clear exploitation. It is much harder and more subtle to observe the growing willingness to engage in self-exploitation.

Excessive Work and Self-Exploitation

What is self-exploitation? Self-exploitation is the voluntary use of energy and time in excess of contractually agreed degrees, often in unhealthy ways. Today many people sacrifice their mental and physical well-being, their family, and their private life in order to advance their professional career.

Many companies and even whole industries are based on the principle of self-exploitation. Most well-known consulting firms,

---

6. Translated from Pali by Thanissaro Bhikkhu.

law firms, and investment banks ask for complete commitment of their junior staff. Eighty-hour work weeks and more are considered standard.

Financial models developed by the economic elite initiated a considerable acceleration and densification of work processes in the last few decades. A new work ethos radically rebuilt our work environments and contributed to an extremely accelerated pace in many areas. It's now considered normal to have high levels of stress and work long hours at work.

When unemployment rises, self-exploitation spreads. Unpaid internships, meagerly paid entry positions, and fierce competition to secure a permanent position or continued employment raise the bar and push many people to their limit.

Recognizing Imbalances

Our working life is in danger of losing its balance. We spend too much time facing screens, working night shifts, managing too many projects simultaneously. We are on call all of the time and take no time for breaks, or for family, friends, exercise, and hobbies.

It reminds me of hearing this story: one day a journalist approached Thich Nhat Hanh. He really liked the master's poetry. Thich Nhat Hanh was working in the garden. The journalist asked why he would attend to the garden himself, as he could write another beautiful poem during that time. Thich Nhat Hanh smiled and said that he could only write poems because he was also a gardener. He could only give his talks because he practiced regular walking meditation. The opposites would balance one another out. Without balance and mindfulness, his life would already have ended.

In the long run, unbalanced working processes will take their toll, and as a result we will suffer mentally and physically. Therefore, it is important to be well aware of the central tensions in our approach to work and to consciously influence them. We need to search for the middle path again and again and defend it against exterior and interior critics.

Moderation in Activities: Concentration of Energy

We hear a lot of talk about work-life balance today. Usually this refers to a situation in which work life and private life are in harmony with each other. But it is not just work and private life that are at stake here. We need to be very clear about the dimensions within our work itself, so we can keep them balanced.

It is important not to lose sight of our own expectations, wishes, hopes, and dreams while we control our aspirations for success, recognition, security, and advancement. As we deal with events, plans, and to-do lists, it is a constant challenge to maintain our mindfulness. We need warning signals when we come close to losing our equilibrium.

Good Timing

Three hours of concentrated, mindful work can result in a more positive outcome than ten hours of work lacking concentration and mindfulness. The essence of our work is often more significant than the number of hours we spend in the office.

Sometimes we struggle, to no avail. The more desperate we are to reach a goal, the farther away it seems. Some things we can't hunt down—they require that we patiently wait for the right moment in time. When we get more familiar with our personal effectiveness, we will be able to fulfill our tasks with less effort and in a shorter time. "The right word at the right time" may cause a miracle to happen. The way of consciously discerning the right approach is taught by many practical examples in Zen circles. A teacher may be able to see a student's deficits in a few minutes. Yet they also know that the student isn't ready yet for the insight into his own mistakes. When the time is appropriate, however, there is only minimal effort needed to attain a transformative effect.

There is also a right time for certain activities. This book was written for the most part in the morning hours of the day. In the morning it is especially easy for me to concentrate. I work effortlessly for three hours with high concentration, and right afterward I experience a steep drop in my concentration, and the quality of my work decreases. I can't increase my work performance by adding more hours. It is up to us to understand which conditions are supportive for what kinds of activities, and where we are only swimming against the current.

Getting Lost in Details: Setting Priorities
Living in balance requires setting priorities. We don't want to waste our precious time with things that aren't important. I know few other stories that makes the importance of priorities clearer than this one:

A teacher brought a number of items to class: a large flower pot, golf balls, small pebbles, and sand. He filled the flower pot up to the top with golf balls and asked the students: "Do you think the pot is full?"

"It is," the students answered.

Then the teacher poured pebbles into the pot until these filled in even the smallest hollow spaces. "Is it full now?" he asked. The students said yes again. Finally the teacher poured sand into the pot until even the tiniest spaces were filled.

"Well, the teacher said, "the flower pot is a symbol for your life. Think of the golf balls as the most important things in your life: your health, your family, your children, your friends. If you had only those and everything else was lost, you would still be immensely rich and live a full life. Think of the pebbles as your house, your car, your work. And the sand symbolizes everything else, like new clothes, home furnishings, a new phone, television. If you fill up the pot with sand first, there won't be room for anything else. The

same goes for your life. When you spend all your energy and time to collect little things, you won't have room for the important things in your life and your life won't be fulfilled. So spend your time and energy on the important things first."

What are our golf balls in the field of work? What is most important to us?

Our work won't provide any true benefit without awareness, without mindfulness, and without empathy. Therefore, it should be our first priority to develop these qualities and maintain them at work.

The first golf ball we place into our workday could be a regular mindfulness practice. This could be sitting meditation at home, a mindful walk to the office, or simply reading something inspiring. Mindfulness will support us to be more effective, to find appropriate solutions, and to be more aware of the emotional dimensions in encounters, meetings, and phone conversations. Mindfulness sows and nurtures mindfulness.

Moderation in Thinking: Moderation in Mental Work

It was only a few decades ago that most of the work in our society was physical labor. Today, however, many of us engage in primarily mental labor. We plan and design, calculate and consult, analyze and formulate, present and discuss, structure and forecast, evaluate, speculate, and much more. Many of us are overwhelmed by the wide range and intensity of the mental processes and impressions we encounter in our daily lives. Our individual and collective minds are strained, and one of the consequences is a sharp rise in psychological, psychosomatic, and stress-related illnesses. Our mind is overwhelmed and tense. Our mental work can get so out of hand that we become detached from our bodies and hardly feel them anymore. Physical exhaustion imposes a natural limit on physical work. Yet mental moderation is hard for us to master. We lack the training.

A seminar participant said the following:

I studied philosophy and have always loved books. I loved think-ing things through passionately. One day I realized that I was constantly thinking. I was thinking without any interruptions. It wasn't an active but rather a passive process. Thoughts ruled me. There was no mechanism to not think consciously. There was no off switch. I didn't come to this insight through intellectual analysis, but rather during a number of sitting meditations at a retreat.

Meditation teachers estimate that more than 95 percent of our daily thoughts are destructive, automatic, and repetitive rather than helpful. Once we also take into consideration that thinking usually consumes 20 percent of our bodily energy, we realize that this is quite wasteful. We are excessive thinkers! Our thinking is not mod-erated. While we have integrated more and more mental activities into our workdays, we haven't mastered the most central mental process: our thinking.

Almost every practitioner of meditation reports the following experience in the beginning of their training: they sit still on their cushion, and their thoughts race in circles. They speculate about the future, and judge the past; they comment, appraise, repeat them-selves, and jump back and forth between all of this thinking. We sit still. There is nothing to do, we have no work, yet our thinking runs at full speed. It is in this moment that we begin to sense the effect that untrained thinking has on our life and on our work. Thinking is action. Thinking makes an impact. Thinking triggers emotions. Thinking creates room for possibilities. Thinking can separate things that belong together. When people meditate over a longer period of time, they learn to observe their thinking with a bit of distance. Then we may realize: non-thinking is possible. Non-thinking creates peace and space. The state of non-thinking can help clear our perception. These are just a few of the insights that regular sitting meditation can give us. We receive a type of catalyst to begin influencing our thinking routines.

Try the following exercise. Sit upright and relaxed in a chair. Place your hand on your lower abdomen, and feel how the abdominal wall moves up and down with the breath. Try to check in with all of your body parts and feel that they are not rigid at all. They are alive. Smile to yourself. Try to devote all of your attention to following your breath during the next five minutes. Counting the individual breaths can serve as an anchor and support our concentration. Breathe in, one, breathe out, one, breathe in, two, breathe out, two. ... When we get lost in our thoughts, we relax, return to our thoughts, and start over at one. When "important thoughts" arise, we let them pass through our mind like a cloud and do not give them any further energy. We can close our eyes and treat ourselves to this five-minute exercise of centering and concentration.

Developing Sensitivity for Warning Signals

When we practice mindfulness by integrating sitting meditation and other practices into our life, we discover a new kind of communication within ourselves. Our body's intelligence awakens. Our physical body constantly sends us messages, but we are rarely ready to receive them. In extreme circumstances, our body will send a signal of distress, yet we often still don't listen. We want our body to function, so that we can continue working uninterrupted. When our physical intelligence is alert and we take our body's signals seriously, we are more in tune with our body's distress calls. We listen to physical signals like fatigue, hunger, ear pressure, and headaches, and also take in our emotional signals. We notice anger rising and the tight feeling of fear growing. Without mindfulness, these states can easily escalate. A minor headache may grow into a strong migraine; a bit of irritation may end in an outburst of rage.

Warning signals remind us to stop and look more closely. Warning signals are the gatekeepers of correct balance.

Non-doing and Leisure

Is it possible for us to take meaningful, nourishing, and restful breaks? Many of us don't remember how to do this, or feel guilty because we might fall behind at work. In some work cultures, taking breaks is frowned on, interpreted as a weakness or even laziness. This is a critical misunderstanding. Taking a break instead of pushing on provides us with space that holds freshness, openness, and mental clarity.

We can't uphold our mindfulness unless we learn to take real breaks. We need to be capable of doing nothing sometimes. Activity needs leisure.

Leisure and activity are two sides of one coin. They are siblings. Every activity requires non-action. Speaking requires silence. Making plans requires time when there is no planning. Every fast-paced phase in our lives requires time to recover. If we let things be, many answers come by themselves. If we keep restlessly chasing after things, they will often escape us. An Indian yoga teacher I met was once very surprised when he attended a tightly organized yoga conference without any breaks. "If you plan everything," he said, "nothing will happen." We may plan, but then we miss unforeseeable opportunities.

If we deliberately refrain from doing, refrain from activities, let go of expectations, we create space. And we need space to experience that which is essential in life. We need space to refresh, space for the unplanned to move in. We need space for ourselves. Space for themes, emotions, tensions, and joys that we missed during the fast flow of life's events. We need space to grow. Leisure is by no means an invitation to deliberately refrain from doing something important. It is often the attitude of non-doing that makes it possible for us to chart new, creative paths and find solutions. Leisure helps us to develop nonreactivity and to escape the need for action, which we often simply imagine. We can smile and clearly state: "No, I do not need to." The spirit of leisure and the spirit of non-doing gifts us with freedom.

If we are no longer able to enjoy doing nothing, if we have a hard time sitting quietly on a chair without being productive, we can be sure that our life is out of balance. We are in danger of losing our true home and drown in our many activities. When we have reached this point, it is time to connect once more with the simplicity of the present moment. We can quietly sit on a chair, breathe deeply three times, and say to ourselves, as Thich Nhat Hanh urges: "I have arrived; I am home." Please indulge in this joy.

Taking a Non-Business Day

It is good to treat oneself to a time-out, so we don't lose our inner compass in the tide of events. Thich Nhat Hanh suggests taking up the ritual of a regular Non-Business Day:

> We should live as free human beings. If we are simply servants of our businesses and our work, we can't be free. We are intelligent enough to realize that we need to dedicate time to ourselves and to our family. However, we can't do it. We can't implement our insight because we are weak on our own. We need friends, fellow practitioners, teachers, and a community to help us face our true problems. Three or four of us can come together and plan a mindfulness day. During this day we teach ourselves to live deeply in every moment. We won't permit our work to occupy our mind and enslave us. We can call this mindfulness day a "non-business day." It is a day when we can be free of worries and don't give in to our tendency of dreaming about the future. It is a day beyond work. [7]

A day like this, which could also be referred to as a leisure day, is a huge challenge for people, and not only for those who work a lot. It is difficult to go through a day without a to-do list, without any plans, and to truly be present throughout the day. We are accustomed to

---

7. Thich Nhat Hanh, Dharma talk during a retreat for business people in Plum Village, fall 1999.

acting according to a plan. When we let the day unfold naturally, we find ourselves in a place beyond schedules. We open up to whatever is happening within us and around us.

Motivation at Work

What drives me? What do I work toward? What are my goals? What is it that gives meaning and fulfillment to my work? What motivates me? Whom does my work serve?

Every human has deep motivation. We have conscious or unconscious goals, a passion or a dream. This deep motivation is very powerful in our life, even if we are not often conscious of it. Deep inside ourselves we have this powerful stream that assesses and prioritizes all our tasks. How much do we know about our true motivation? I was misled for many years because I didn't understand my true motivation.

Frankfurt, December 1997, McKinsey Selection Interviews. I am attending the final meeting after I passed an intelligence test, solved several case studies, and delivered a presentation. It is time for the inevitable question: "Why do you want to work for us?" My answer is right out of the textbook. I want to work with intelligent people, I want to pursue a stellar career, and I believe this is the right environment. I had my own positive experiences in-house and have heard many good things about the company from active consultants and partners. I want to be part of meaningful projects. I am willing to ignore the terrible experience I had with my thesis, which I wrote right here in this company, an experience which brought me to the brink of a mental and physical breakdown. Nonetheless, I want to be part of it! I am not in touch with my deeper motivation.

It was years later, sitting on a meditation cushion, that I understood what really led me to McKinsey. I wanted to prove to myself and to others that I had "made it." I was fascinated by the intellectual dominance that I saw in many of the consultants. I wanted the permanent mark of professional success on my CV. I longed for belonging, recognition, and mutual support. I wanted a secure home. And I wanted to make a lot of money so that I could become independent as soon as possible.

Are we aware of our deepest motivation? Do we know what guides and directs our life on the deepest level? Are we trying to gain clarity about our unconscious goals and what we might unconsciously avoid? Without this clarity, our work lacks direction. We are never truly free. We are easily seduced and manipulated. Other people can connect with our unconscious wishes and hopes to take us along.

Behind the Shining Facades

These statements are revolutionary, yet not by any means new. They are revolutionary because they can change the direction of our lives in a way that differs fundamentally from the predominant popular culture. We witness the current financial and economic crisis and see where the yearning for quick money, career, fame, and power can lead. But we won't let go of the old concept. We continue to look for a career that will grant us more money, greater recognition, more influence and fame.

Here in Germany, the media keeps looking for the next superstar in a popular TV-show called *Who wants to be the next millionaire?* So many people seem fascinated by celebrities and are keen to follow their every minor move. There is hardly any advertisement we encounter that doesn't play into our desires for money, beauty, youth, sensual pleasure, power, and fame. But these are false promises.

University of Geneva, January 1998. I am defending my doctoral thesis, titled: "Organization through the Lens of the Knowledge Process." I researched this topic for three years, wrote intensely about it, immersed myself in it, and breathed it. In preparation for my PhD, I polished my meager French in a two-week crash course. Now I face the examiners and start. I feel fear; my French limits me a lot. My goal is summa cum laude. The highest distinction. I succeed. People congratulate me. I've worked toward this goal for three years. I made it. What now? Nothing happens. I feel very, very tired. I'm still the same person. What did I expect? I've reached the goal, forced myself to get there; I succeeded. Yet I'm not any happier. I completed my PhD, sure. Am I calmer, more content, more capable of loving? There is disappointment. What do I really want? My success is fading already and I'm aware of the next mountains of struggle rising from the depths of my consciousness. I will move from Zürich to Hamburg; I need to renovate my apartment and will start a new job in four months. This is an endless cycle that I play along with.

We hear so many promises. "This will make you happy!" "This will give you security!" "This will help you develop further." With mindfulness we will be able to see whether these promises are true. We will be able to see through the facade of success. We see the fear that might hide behind a confident smile. We are aware of the loneliness and depression many important figures experience. The rich and famous have a difficult time finding friends they can trust. They also lose the ability to move freely through their daily lives. Maintaining a public image takes great effort. Wealth, prominence, power, and fame come at a price, and once a certain status has been achieved, the fear of losing it again follows. When we approach these drawbacks with greater clarity, we find the same processes and modes of action within ourselves. This insight can change our motivation. We will not let ourselves be fooled any longer.

Misguided Incentives

When we analyze the motivational structures followed by companies and economic players, we gain deeper insights. What are the motivators used in incentive programs, promoting junior employees, motivational seminars and career counseling? What is the driving source of motivation for board members or management personnel? If the answer is fame, money, and power, it will lead to problems for customers, citizens, and all of society. If we work for these organizations, we will be influenced by these motivations day in and day out and won't be able to escape them.

We should be aware of the type of carrot that is dangling in front of us. Incentive structures of organizations reflect the way human beings are viewed by their leaders. If we know what we are living and working for, we don't need to be motivated. I'm not denying that every human needs recognition and some support. If we only work, however, to receive acknowledgment, we are on a path that leads to dependency and a lack of freedom.

For years, management in large corporations attracted employees with stock options and other profit-oriented incentives. These reward systems were the most common motivational mechanisms in the financial sector, especially prevalent with investment bankers and widespread among large stock corporations. The transfer of performance standards to the markets led to the collective irresponsibility that we encountered during the financial crisis of 2008. Some typical answers of investment bankers confronted with their responsibility for the crisis might be:

"I didn't do it."

"It was the market."

"An unforeseeable accident."

"A few people discredited a whole industry."

"I'm also a victim of this crisis."

But looking deeply, we can see this "accident" was no accident at all, but rather the manifestation of a system built on unwholesome motivational principles which continue to be applied.

Radical Honesty

The realm of motivation is subtle. There is no other area where it is easier to delude ourselves. Here is the experience of a management coach:

> *It is my main job to help my clients to see themselves as they are. I can only help them if they are honest with themselves. In the beginning there is often a wall of self-deception and distorted perception. A top executive I met with insisted for weeks that his main motivation was the well-being of his family, and in reality he hardly ever saw his wife and children and was about to go through a divorce. If we cannot break through this wall, nothing will change. We simply stay on the surface and move some furniture around. As soon as radical self-honesty comes in, we enter a new terrain and everything can change.*

We can only get to radical honesty when we pay close attention to the motivators that provoke either great enthusiasm or strong denial in us.

Deep Work Motivation	Response Patterns
money	income level, returns, financial gains and losses, changes in the volume of assets, fees
fame	professional recognition, praise, decorations, honors, media reports
power	resources, influence, proximity to powerful people, control options, leverage
sensual pleasures	pleasant and unpleasant scents, views, sounds, tastes, and touch
sex	signals by potential partners, attractiveness, desirability

Table 3: Work motivations and response patterns

Mindfulness helps us to recognize our "buttons" and the ideas that drive our behavior. We can only apply a meaningful strategy when we understand what we are striving toward. If fame, power, wealth, sex, or sensual pleasure in their different variants motivate our actions, we can observe how reaching any of these goals disappoints us time and time again. A friend who meditated for a long time told me about his process:

Mindfulness helps us recognize the true nature of our motivation. It will help us to let go of orientation patterns that won't lead us toward a fulfilled life.

Clarity through Crisis

Many different life events may help us shed misconceptions and harmful life strategies. The most dramatic, most radical, and most effective way is a crisis. A crisis is defined as a problematic decision-making process linked to a turning point. It may be triggered by internal or external factors. We might become severely ill, lose our partner, or barely escape death. In the context of work, a crisis is often triggered by burnout, depression, a heart attack, or other illnesses, but also by terminations and professional setbacks. During the escalation of a crisis we understand that our old life needs to change radically. We stand in front of a wall.

Crises may be very painful, yet as long as they don't destroy us, they can accelerate our development. Crises can open us to new possibilities. A crisis does away with what we thought was "normal." Self-images, opinions, priorities, judgments, and fundamental orientations go up in flames. We are open for the new. In a certain sense we are reborn.

After the gate in the wall opens up, the growth process that will sustain and strengthen new motivations can start. This may take years. Determination, a positive environment, and systematic mental training will support the process.

Developing and Strengthening Wholesome Motivations

Fame, power, wealth, sex, and sensual pleasures aren't intrinsically bad in themselves, but they are unsuitable as guideposts through our lives. They lead us astray. The Buddha showed alternatives to these five unwholesome forms of motivation. He recommended that we seek refuge with the spirit of love and compassion, also called bodhicitta. Bodhicitta is the deep and boundless desire to understand and to love. It is the need felt to strive empathy and compassion for the benefit of oneself and all other beings.

Experiencing and Sustaining the Strength of Bodhicitta

It is not easy to identify our deepest motivation or to admit that we use our work to gain more recognition and praise. It is hard to admit that we strive for influence and more money. We may easily delude ourselves. When we sit down to meditate, however, and train our mind, we gain greater clarity regarding our true driving forces.

The historical Buddha was very successful at a young age. He was young, athletic, handsome, highly intelligent, and had been educated by the best teachers of his time. He was a prince with access to power and owned palaces and riches. He had everything. And yet he left behind this life that most people see as highly desirable and consciously or unconsciously strive for.

Siddhartha realized that he couldn't develop inner freedom in his privileged position. He saw that everything he owned was impermanent. He realized he would lose his youth, that his body might fall ill, and that he would finally, eventually, die. The power he currently held was not a secure foundation; it had to be defended again and again. He realized that it was his task to dissolve the suffering within himself and that consumption, success, and praise could only mask it, not help to overcome it. He became an ascetic and went on a six-year intense training odyssey, traveling to many different meditation teachers. At one point, he almost starved to death in the woods of India. On this journey he found a path to overcome suffering: the path we call Buddhadharma today. He learned that we need to awaken the spirit of love within, for the well-being of ourselves and for others, so that we can move our life's direction toward peace, happiness, and wisdom. When we choose Bodhicitta as our life's deepest motivation, we direct ourselves and our environment onto a wholesome path. It was the Buddha's deepest wish to awaken the spirit of love and enlightenment in others, a motivation that allowed him to connect with people of all religions, persuasions, professions, and castes.

Compassion in the Office: Staying in Contact
Compassion does not come naturally to all of us. It is hard for us to wish people well who we find unsympathetic, who have hurt us, or to whom we feel distant from. We need to practice compassion.

If we can overcome the inner separation from our clients, colleagues, subcontractors, investors, and supervisors, we can make new connections and even the path for a new beginning. How do we practice compassion? Loving kindness meditation, also called Metta meditation, is a proven method that allows us to send positive wishes first to ourselves, then to dear friends and family members, and finally in ever-widening circles: to people we see as neutral, to difficult people, and even to our enemies. We focus our mind and say internally, silently: "May you be happy," "May you be content," and similar blessings.

Here is the testimony of a retreat participant:

Half a year ago, I got a new boss, and right from the beginning we had difficulties working together. As soon as we were in the same room, I felt tense. We had many misunderstandings and conflicts. About a month ago, I started including my boss in my Metta meditation. Every morning I wish him and myself well. I wish that we won't give in to anger and impatience. After only a few days, my relationship with my boss changed. There was way less tension. Our relationship has changed for the better. It was like a miracle.

Below you will find a classic Metta meditation that you can dedicate to yourself, to your supervisor, to a colleague, or someone else. For this example, I've used my boss.

Metta Meditation for the Working Life

Sit upright and comfortably on a cushion or chair and focus on your in-breath and your out-breath. Simply enjoy your breath for the next couple of minutes. Then begin to repeat the sentences below. You might coordinate reciting the sentences with your breath or simply let them sink into your mind:

May my boss be peaceful, happy, and at ease in body and mind.

May my boss be free of hurt and grievance.

May my boss be free of anger, confusion, fear, and anxiety.

May my boss learn to look at himself with the eyes of love and understanding.

May my boss be able to see and touch the seeds of joy and happiness within.

May my boss learn to discern the sources of anger, craving, and delusion within.

———

May my boss experience how to feed the seeds of joy every day.

May my boss be able to live solidly and freely.

May my boss be free of attachment and rejection.

The regular practice of Metta meditation submerges our mind in goodwill as we emit positive thoughts and good wishes into our environment. Metta meditation is food and fertilizer for kind, peaceful, harmonious, and constructive encounters. In difficult situations and when we deal with difficult people, Metta meditation helps us to avoid separation and maintain contact with one another. Metta meditation, practiced conscientiously, can be much more effective than expensive team development seminars and coaching sessions.

Looking for the Noble Core (Goodness) in People

You may have heard the phrase "a self-fulfilling prophecy." The stronger our expectation for a certain outcome is, the more likely it will come to pass. An old proverb states: "What you shout into the woods, will echo back." Our view of humanity has a remarkable effect in this context. Our expectations of those we encounter will influence how they behave toward us. The power of our mind is huge. Our conception of the human being leads us to manifest our own world.

> *Switzerland, summer 2006. I am in charge of a stress-reduction seminar in a large company. I didn't sleep well, and I feel weak and a bit groggy. As I survey the room, the seminar participants are eyeing me critically, even with hostility. I become tense. My competitiveness is awakened. I observe myself quickly creating a few clever sentences to show off my competence. A phone rings in the distance, I wake from my thoughts. What am I doing right now? All seminar participants have the potential of becoming Buddhas. In my thoughts, however, I view them as enemies. I smile to myself and reconnect. I take another look at the participants. Their faces have changed. I see that shine in their eyes. The separation is gone. Now I can start.*

Buddhism gives us a realistic and optimistic view of humanity. Experienced teachers agree that our mind tends to be confused by wrong views and ideas. Therefore, it can easily fall under the guidance of unwholesome mental states. If we untangle these knots, our true nature can shine through. Our true nature is radiant, kind, and full of peace. When I see my colleagues as competitors, power struggles will happen. If I suspect that I can't trust them, they will prove me right. If I see my colleagues, however, as companions on the path, as potential Buddhas, everything changes.

In Plum Village, I learned how to bow to others. I would say to myself: "A lotus for you, a Buddha to be." This is a powerful exercise. It is hard to hang on to a negative image of another person when we bow to him or her in this spirit. When I am able to focus on the noble core in another human, no matter how difficult the person might be, our relationship will change enormously. If I can maintain the positive contact, wholesome change can begin. We sabotage our relationships as long as we can't let go of prejudices, negative images, or a destructive image of humankind.

Many of us lack confidence in the noble core and humankind's positive potential. We lack confidence in our radiant human nature. We lack confidence in our spiritual power and developmental capacities. A member of the Network for Mindful Business explained:

> *I used to view my colleagues as competitors. Some of them I even actively disliked. Mindfulness practice taught me how I harm myself when I see others negatively. I try hard to soften this deeply rooted view of humanity in my work meditations. I have noticed how my face freezes and how my jaw gets rigid during work hours. Whenever I look at my colleagues with kinder eyes, I receive a lot of appreciation and positive feedback.*

We love it when people see our good sides. We blossom when others don't jump to conclusions about us. A positive view of humanity fosters a positive self-image. We recognize our potential, and our willingness to develop systematically through training our mind grows.

Input Focus instead of Output Focus

If we strive for external success, reaching goals is very important to us. Our guideposts are external milestones: budget figures, election results, placements, evaluations, reports, credentials, and more. Results are what counts.

We can't control our successes entirely, however. We have already shown how foolhardy it is to take an event out of its multifaceted context and claim it for ourselves, to say "I did this." It might be wiser to focus more on the actual input, rather than spending too much time on future results (the output). That can relax our life a lot and bring us great happiness.

We start with the factors we can influence. We pay attention to our motivation and the fragrance of our spirit. Sometimes we give everything and we have nothing to show for it. Other times we don't put in much effort at all and collect success after success. As long as we focus on our input, we are on the safe side. We won't be tossed around by exterior forces. During times of failure we remain persistent. In times of success we don't need to act conceited.

Transcending the Three Complexes

The Buddha spoke of three complexes of the spirit, which arise when we compare ourselves to others unmindfully. Comparisons, in a vacuum, are neither good nor bad. Comparisons can provide us with some necessary information. Most of the time, however, we are quick to add a judgment to the comparison. This is the origin of the three complexes.

Superiority Complex

The first disease of the comparing mind is the belief that we are superior to others (the superiority complex). When we feel superior, we are convinced that we are better than others and that we deserve more than they do.

We are all susceptible to this complex. It all depends on how much we define ourselves by the rank we hold in a given group. What are the dimensions we use to compare ourselves to others? How do we deal with people who are not quite as capable or efficient as we are in one area or another? I'm quite familiar with the superiority complex, based on my own experience. As I went to university and was a high achiever, I built up a certain perception of myself. Only after I started practicing mindfulness did I realize what kind of sweet poison I had enjoyed with pleasure for years. I saw that there is a high price to pay for feeling superior and condescending. When we feel superior to others, we separate ourselves from them. And if we want to uphold our superior position, we have to prove ourselves over and over again. It's a vicious cycle that can lead to unhappiness.

Inferiority

The second disease of the comparing mind is the conviction or judgment that we are worth less than others (the inferiority complex). If we believe this, we will also believe that we deserve less than others, that it is okay if we are treated worse. We regard those we feel inferior to with fearful or admiring eyes.

Every single human has their weak points. We might be excellent in many areas and still suffer from feelings of inferiority. Superiority and inferiority need each other. They are two sides of the same coin.

Equality

The third disease of the comparing mind is the conviction or judgment that I am just the same as another person, and that we are all equal (the equality complex). Maybe I'm really convinced that I deserve the same as others. I might believe that it is my right to be treated in the same way as someone else.

Yet we know that when we look closely, no human being is exactly like another. No two things are exactly the same. The idea of equality is an idea that we won't find anywhere either within or outside ourselves. If we look deeply into any two things in the world, we will always find that they are different in some way. The idea of equality can cause a lot of suffering.

Beyond Praise and Blame

The three complexes are very closely interconnected, and they permeate all work processes. Competition and rivalry are the guiding principles in many companies; they create winners and losers on a daily basis. Measuring performance and getting ahead are the driving forces behind our market economy. If all this constant comparison is done without mindfulness, we find ourselves on a slippery slope.

As humans, we have the gift of thinking and analyzing. This gift, however, is a double-edged sword. Unless we are mindful of our comparisons, they will become a source of anxiety, frustration, unhappiness, and division for ourselves and others. It is exhausting to constantly compare oneself with others. It robs us of peace, energy, and joy, and distracts from the unity of life.

body, nation, age, sports

health, muscles, children, success

clothing, income, money, school, popularity

car, intelligence, attractiveness, degree, ethics

love, manners, power, origin, house, assets

Illustration 9: Dimensions of the comparing complex

Beyond Competitive Thinking

It is possible to reach a place that lies beyond competitive thinking. The prerequisite is to calm one's mind.

A participant reported after an event:

After watching my breath for two days and developing mindfulness throughout my body, my thinking slowed down. Previously there was an uninterrupted stream of associations, ideas, and judgments, but now my mind becomes clearer and clearer, and I can see individual thoughts and judgments more distinctly. I see thoughts rise up like soap bubbles and burst. It can be frightening what kind of thoughts my mind comes up with. I learned not to take my thoughts so seriously anymore. Sometimes my thinking stops completely. Then I feel extremely peaceful and connected to everything.

It is important to reinforce this spirit of connectedness. Our economic system, with its emphasis on competitive thinking, strengthens that which separates and compares. We need to learn that we don't have to sacrifice the spirit of connectedness on the altar of economics.

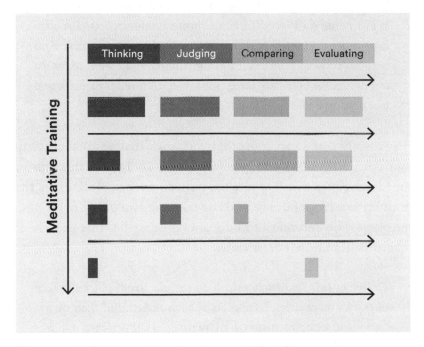

Illustration 10: Calming and moderating central thought processes

Competition has become second nature to many of us. We are used to being evaluated and graded from an early age. Our lives will benefit when we can free ourselves from competitive thinking.

I Am Not My Work, I Am Not My Success

In general, people who are completely immersed in and devoted to their work are looked upon positively in our society. They found their calling, the work is fulfilling, and they are good at it. Yet every identification also includes a limitation, and can lead to suffering. We are always a lot more than our work.

The suffering we experience when we lose our job reflects the degree to which we hold on and are attached to it.

> *June 1998, Hamburg. After I hand in my resignation at Mc-Kinsey, my whole identity and self-esteem slowly begin to collapse. Who am I if I'm not working for a big company like McKinsey? What value do I have if I can't show visible success? I realize how much I identify with my successes. I am my success. And without success? Who am I? I am shrinking and I want to return to my success. I created an ego for myself that relies on work and work success. I have never felt so bad before.*

The insight that we are more than our work, that we are more than our opinions, habits, and beliefs, can free us. To gain that type of freedom requires insight into the impermanence of all things, the mutual interdependence and the coming and going of all phenomena. The Zen master Kodo Sawaki describes this process of identification rather drastically:

> *To live in this floating world is to wander from place to place pursuing mere titles. Each of us is born naked. But then we are given a name and registered. We're covered with clothes, a nipple is stuffed into our mouth, and so on. When we grow up, people say,*

"This person is great, strong, clever, rich." We find consolation in words, when in fact everyone is simply naked.[8]

What is the relationship between my work and the rest of my life? How much do I identify with my work? Who am I when I am no longer working? Our mind tends to gravitate toward identification—in Buddhism, we would call it attachment. Instead of thinking: "Yes, I do have work in my life," we think: "I am my work." This identification is highly dangerous. When we are too closely attached to our work we create a variety of problems.

Conscious Weakening of the EGO

When we define ourselves in terms of our work, we are building an "ego" that is dependent on work. This identification process can have deep implications: "This was *me*." "I did this." "This is *my* staff." "This was *my* idea." The first person comes easily in our language. I (the ego) collect convictions, objects, habits, character traits, and many other things that define me (the ego).

During meditation, the ego is revealed as an illusion. It is a non-real identification point (*manas*) that sends its disrupting signals into all areas of our being. The famous German nun Ayya Khema once expressed the amazing insight: "Without me, life is easy." Our ego is a troublemaker. It will always place us in the center, where we get in the way of everyone else. Our ego makes constant claims on us, needs to be protected, and has difficulties accepting the constant changes inside and outside. If we take refuge in the self, we seek refuge in rigidity, separation, and conflict.

In this condition, everything in the world is an object for us. Everything can become an object because we experience separation on a very deep level. Therefore, it makes sense to maximize our personal gain and develop different strategies to do so. We emphasize

8. Kosho Uchiyama Roshi, *The Zen Teaching of Homeless Kodo* (Boston: Wisdom Publications, 2014).

our individuality—our differences. We overestimate our power when we are doing well or our responsibility when we are doing poorly. Zen master Uchiyama Roshi gives the following example:

> When the president of a big company that has constructed several large buildings thinks that he built those, he makes a gross mistake. He simply happened to be at the head of the company when many different forces cooperated closely to finish a building. He couldn't even have made one reinforced iron bar by himself. Modern people just engage in a tug of war: they compete for illusionary power high up in the clouds of their social system. The system might appear to be solid, but it is transient, like clouds.[9]

Our individualism, our separation, run so deep in us that we mostly don't even notice it. When I lived in Plum Village, which is strongly Vietnamese-influenced, I was surprised how easily new arrivals became integrated into the existing web of personal and work relations. They swam along, they followed the schools of fish, yet they also appeared to be themselves. I found this irritating. It didn't come easily to me. When I attempted to imitate them, I noticed that while I tried to *follow* the group (separation of object and subject), the others actually *were* the group (unity of object and subject).

Many meditation centers aim at the conscious weakening of our ego. During longer periods of sitting, we concentrate on the impermanence of all objects of our body and mind. Moment by moment we experience the transformation of all being and recognize that there is no object with a solid, everlasting core. All things are empty, the Heart Sutra says. Our ego is a self-constructed illusion that causes problems. This insight can free our mind and make it more flexible.

Selling Ourselves No Longer: How to Maintain Our Integrity

When we have valuable talents, publicity, influence potentials, or

---

9. Ibid.

abilities, others will want to use our services, our name, and our influence. This is especially easy to observe in the realm of sports. Not much time passes before the faces of gold-medal winners and world champions grace ads for chocolate, cars, sausages, financial services, shampoo, and beer.

Our personal integrity and credibility are of high value to our work. Even more important than outer integrity is our inner integrity, which is reflected in the absence of discrepancies between word and deed, inside and outside, professional ideals and personal life. Grumpy nuns, arrogant preachers, and trade unionists addicted to luxury are tragic figures, walking paradoxes. But beyond those extreme examples, many of us struggle with very unrealistic exterior and interior aspirations that we cannot live up to.

Mindfulness helps us to end the struggle within ourselves. We do not need to judge ourselves so harshly. We can learn to accept our weaknesses and, at the same time, to do something about them.

Understanding the Motivation of Our Environment

One of the greatest misunderstandings in the field of motivation is that an individual, unwholesome motivation can still result in a collective positive wholesome outcome. As an example, it is the belief that a company that acts greedily could create something positive for the whole of society by creating jobs, its contribution to the gross national product, and its tremendous energetic drive.

It is common practice and is still valid in many economic and business contexts to ignore the motivation for economic actions. I remember a personal confrontation I had with the dean of a well-known department of economics. Both of us were participants in a symposium, and exchanged views on corporate ethics in a study group. I presented my thoughts on the tremendous influence of one's personal motivation on the effect of an action. I said that no action could be isolated from the underlying motivation. Two people who want to help someone will obtain very different results depending on the ethics of their motivation. I believe that it is essential to discuss these connections at universities. My presentation aggravated the business administration professor so much that he retorted angrily: "I don't care about the motivation of my students at all. The main thing is that they do something, whether that be for their CV, their career, or any other reason. They get credit for that. Research based on motivation is a dreadful thing."

I believe that the inner dimension of our economic motivation, the active analysis of wholesome and unwholesome motivations, presents a great opportunity for universities and businesses.

Clarifying Time-out

Sometimes it is simply not enough to take a personal day off. There are times when we need a longer time-out. We need to gain distance from our day-to-day life and work routine. We need to be free from daily chores. The classical vacation can only create this distance to a certain extent. During a vacation we don't usually confront our everyday life—we are trying to get away from it all. We don't necessarily receive clarity and insight.

Going on a retreat is a better way to gain mental clarity. A retreat is a planned withdrawal from our everyday life from a few days up to a few months. Retreats offer a strict daily schedule that is designed to allow for clarity and rest. Many different spiritual practices offer such phases of contemplation and withdrawal.

Winter Retreat, 2001, Plum Village. I joined a group of fifteen 15 men who attend the three-month winter retreat together. Our days are tightly structured: we practice sitting, walking, eating, and work meditation. We gather together on a regular basis to talk about our experiences. We talk with great openness and honesty, which is a touching experience for us and highly instructive. We look deep into our lives, and our habits, and we receive inspiration and clarity.

Nowadays, it is not too unusual for people to take a longer time-out, a so called sabbatical. These out times are especially transformative when we allow ourselves to step into an undefined space without any fixed expectations regarding the results. Without any follow-up contract or guarantee of a job, we allow ourselves to open up to the real themes, values, fears, and hopes in our lives. I have met several people who emerged renewed and invigorated from such phases.

Serving Meaningful Purposes

We don't feel right when our work doesn't serve a useful purpose. It is not without reason that wise elders often talk about the joy of selfless service and warn about egocentricity, selfishness, and egotism. Catastrophes, such as earthquakes, hurricanes, and tsunamis, regularly provoke a huge outpouring of support. People who join the relief teams might undergo a change in their lives; by helping others, we can let go of the burden of our ego.

To help others is part of our true human nature. However, we might be afraid that there won't be anything left when we share ourselves and our work with everyone. The more we let this reluctance and fear imprison us, the poorer are our communities.

We are no saints. Yet this doesn't mean that we can't strive to become saints. We are not selfless—we are often governed by selfish motives. This doesn't mean, however, that we can't train our selflessness. We can do it step-by-step and without any false holiness.

Just as in the practice of Metta meditation, we can aim for our work to contribute to wider and wider circles. We start with our personal livelihood: we work for our families, we take care of friends and neighbors, and ultimately try to dedicate our work to all humans, even all beings. The work of Jesus and of many wise people throughout human history knew no bounds. There are role models who we needn't shy away from, but whom we can emulate with honest effort and as well as we can.

Deep down inside ourselves, we know whether we serve a

meaningless or a meaningful cause. We find out when we sit quietly on a chair and connect to our present work. How do we feel? Do we feel narrow or wide? Fearful or peaceful? Angry or happy? Tense or relaxed? What should the inscription on our tombstone say? Our actions are our true legacy in this life. The confrontation with the quality and purpose of these actions can encourage us to open our hearts.

We Are the Money

We are the economy. We are the ones who created the economy, and we are the ones recreating it daily anew. With this in mind, it is worthwhile to illuminate and examine our personal relationship to the issue of money.

Everybody talks about money. Philosophers and entrepreneurs through history have had plenty of insights:

> *"Money is like seawater: the more we drink, the thirstier we become."*
> —Arthur Schopenhauer

> *"A business that makes nothing but money is a poor business."*
> —Henry Ford

> *"Make money your God and it will plague you like the devil."*
> —Henry Fielding

> *"Money may be the husk of many things, but not the kernel.*
> *It brings you food, but not appetite; medicine, but not health;*
> *acquaintances, but not friends; servants, but not loyalty;*
> *days of joy, but not peace or happiness."*
> —Henrik Ibsen

We cannot ignore money. The invention of money made a fundamental impact on our society and culture. Money is a lot more than a universal medium or means of exchange and store of value. Money permeates our spiritual world, our innermost being.

We work for money and we shop with money. We lend, save, and invest. If we look into it carefully, our relationship with money can become an expression and mirror of our attitude toward life.

When we lift the abstract veil of money, we can see the true nature of the economic processes and our individual needs and understand our motivations more clearly. Money offers us a huge projection surface for many of our unfulfilled desires.

Our monthly audit of our bank account, checking the bill at the restaurant, taking out a life insurance policy, and contributing to a charity are all expressions of our perception of money. Our perception of money becomes an expression of the things we take to be true in relation to our money.

Money seems to hold a universal key to security, power, and control—maybe even to personal happiness. A part of us, however, knows that this isn't true.

The Mysterious Energy of Money
In our economic system, money is energy. It would be helpful to understand this energy and channel it wholesomely. During recent years, however, money has been channeled in unwholesome ways. Money is no longer connected to the real economy.

Hiddensee, Germany, February 2009. Writing retreat. After spending the whole day on the subject of money, I watch the news. The topics are almost exclusively on financial and economic events. The bailout of Hypo Real Estate, plant closures at Opel, Obama's stimulus package, the bankruptcy of Qimonda, statements on economic developments by the finance minister and the German chancellor. It is all about money, money, and more money. The question of money is everywhere and dominates everything.

The subject of money has taken on a life of its own. It controls our attention. Money offers a projection screen for our unfulfilled desires.

When money pours into our lives, our possibilities seem to multiply. Attachment to money and possessions is often described as a source of problems in Buddhism. Attachment is at the root of greed ("I want this!") and refusal ("I don't want this!"). The Buddha teaches that we are a lot more than what we own or spend. Money and monetary processes, however, penetrate day-to-day life. They structure central areas of our life and our work. We work for money and we shop with money. We lend, save, and invest. The true nature of economic processes and our genuine needs can disappear behind the abstract veil of money. How can we see and act more clearly in this area?

The Buddha and Money

The Buddha didn't own any money. He taught and wandered as a monk throughout India—he had no possessions. Born as a prince, he took off his crown and left all his wealth behind to explore the roots of human suffering and happiness. He taught time and time again that it wasn't worth it to become a slave to money or possessions. He demonstrated how we can free ourselves from wrong ideas and perceptions by the persistent practice of mindfulness, ethics, and generosity. Through this practice, we can reach peace and happiness.

The Buddha and his students showed that we can be happy and content with fewer financial resources. We can cultivate a wholesome relationship with money and property. In a society that sees growth as the solution to every problem, we need greater clarity in our own life to avoid being caught up in the mainstream.

We can ask ourselves what money represents in our lives. What do we expect from material success? How often during the day do our thoughts wander to the subject of money? What kind of inner dialogues are set off? A financial cushion may allow us to be not quite as keenly aware of our existential vulnerability. We are vulnerable as human beings. We will get sick, we will grow old, and we all die. Knowing that, is it still possible to live a happy life?

The Buddha teaches that it is possible, when we cultivate our mindfulness and look deeply into our genuine needs. The need to love and to understand is a much better guide than the pursuit of power, money, and fame.

We connect anew with all things and beings in our environment. We pause and observe all our impulses telling us to consume without having to act upon them. As we touch the many small miracles of life, we become freer.

A more mindful relationship with money and possessions has many positive effects for society. We can channel our financial energies into more beneficial areas. We can deprive destructive products, companies, and mind-sets of energy. The way we use money on a daily basis is a demonstration of our values and real needs.

The Dalai Lama Answers Questions about Money

The Dalai Lama formulated eight helpful questions about the right way of dealing with money and wealth:[10]

1. Did you gain your wealth rightfully?
2. Has your wealth benefitted you alone?
3. Has your wealth made others happy?
4. Have you shared your wealth with others?
5. Have you done good deeds with your wealth?
6. Are you attached to your wealth? Are you in love with it?
7. Are you aware of the dangers of wealth?
8. Do you have the knowledge leading to spiritual freedom?

What are your answers?

These questions should not be read as a moral request. They arise from deep insight. If we don't share our wealth, we become separated from the world. We become separated from all the joy that arises when we help others. Our society wastes its prosperity if it is not shared in the right way.

---

10. The Dalai Lama, *The Leader's Way* (New York: Broadway Books, 2009).

It makes a lot of sense to meditate on our relationship to money, even when it gives us a headache. As I've thought about mindful economic activity, the subject of money has been particularly difficult. It was easy for me to buy organic eggs and resign from my meaningless job. But I found it very difficult to look openly and honestly into my own ways of relating to money.

Hereafter, we will consider the financial dimension of our life from the perspective we are now familiar with. We are looking at

- the fragrance of our money and our possessions.

- the true nature of money and wealth.

- the correct balance and the right means.

- our expectations of money, our deepest motivation, and our inner and external drivers in the field of finances.

The Fragrance of Money: Money Is Spirit

In the chapter about mindful work, we saw how much depends on the mind-set we inhabit as we go about our work. The same is true for our money. A dollar isn't the same as any other dollar. My financial transactions are informed by my attitude. If I am angry and full of demands, my financial actions will carry this greed into the world. If my mind is compassionate and patient, my investments will carry the same spirit.

If I was to give someone one hundred dollars, it could make someone very happy, but it could also make a person feel ashamed. The effect the gift has depends on the mind-set of the giver and also on that of the recipient. When we give money in anger, it will foster anger. Money given out of joy will nurture joy.

Money is a powerful energy that flows through our life and reveals our hidden attitudes and leanings. Wanting for more, or having enough. Excessiveness or modesty. Money can reveal our personal states.

What Is the Fragrance of Our Money? What Are Its Qualities?
A hundred-dollar bill can't talk about its long journey through different wallets and cash registers. It passes from hand to hand. It can be used to buy flowers, newspapers, or weapons. It serves criminals and average citizens equally.

There is an old Latin proverb: *Pecunia non olet*, "Money doesn't stink." I would disagree. Money does have a distinct odor. Our motivation, our moods sense it. Every financial transaction is also a spiritual act. Every time we accept, invest, or spend money, there will be an effect. We can't separate our money from its past, present, or future.

Our money holds the scent of everything. Love or hatred. Gratefulness or greed. Shame or freedom. Shared joy or envy. Jealousy or brotherhood. Patience or impatience. Clarity or self-delusion. Restlessness or equanimity.

Every one of these mental states has an influence on the way we handle our money. Every amount of money that we earn, invest, or spend has its specific fragrance.

It is our attitude toward money that makes all the difference.

Berlin, fall 2006. I receive a message that an important client is canceling a series of my seminars due to internal reorganization. My financial plan for the rest of the year collapses. I am fearful and angry. I feel sick all of a sudden. It surprises me how many different things hinge on this particular amount of money. I sit down on my meditation cushion, breathe quietly and watch the inner turmoil. Something important seems to be threatened. My thoughts come up with all sorts of potential worst-case scenarios. After half an hour, I begin to calm down. In the evening, my wife and I talk for a long time about the meaning of money in our lives. We get a clearer picture of our expectations and fears. We realize that we still have many blind spots when it comes to dealing with money.

Qualities of Money

Money is a chameleon, and it adapts to the color of its master. Our day-to-day use of language shows the chameleonlike versatility of money. The role, effect, and quality of our money in the world changes depending on our own state of mind. We transfer our state of mind to our money. Mindfulness helps us to identify these qualities:

Nervous money is easily scared and can disappear in a flash when it feels threatened.

Dirty money comes from unethical or criminal sources.

Cold money: there is no deeper relationship between borrower and intended purpose.

Warm money: there is a deeper relationship between borrower and intended purpose.

Demanding money expects high rates of return.

Patient money pursues long-term plans.

Compassionate money helps where there are needs.

Fast money doesn't care about long-term effects or risks.

Fearful money hides in the background.

Calculating money has a clearly defined use in mind.

Old money has been in the same family for a long time.

Honest money was acquired diligently and by respectable work.

Our money can serve honest or criminal purposes. We should look carefully at the mind-set and motivations behind payments, donations, and investments in our household and in our environment. This will help us to become more aware of the true fragrance of money.

The Fragrance of Our Financial Actions

We can take countless possible actions with our money. And there are two sides to every action. A lender needs a borrower. Whatever I own cannot be owned by another person. My gain may be another person's loss. A landlord needs a renter. All these actions reflect our mental states. I can give items joyfully, with distrust, or in a completely neutral way. The same is true when loaning and receiving things. I may resent every cent I pay to the IRS. Losses can be devastating, or I can accept them as a matter of fact. There are many ways to either waste mental energy or build on it when we are dealing with money.

Financial Action	Fragrance of the Action	Opposite Action	Fragrance of the Opposite Action
giving	How do I give?	taking	How do I take?
gift	How do I give a gift?	receive	How do I receive a gift?
loan	How do I loan?	borrow	How do I borrow?
rent out	How do I rent out?	rent	How do I rent?
sell	How do I sell?	buy	How do I buy?
invest	How or where do I invest?	save	How do I save?
making a loan	How do I make a loan?	taking out a loan	How do I take out a loan?
win	How do I win?	lose	How do I lose?
bequest	How do I bequest?	inherit	How do I inherit?

levy taxes	How are taxes calculated?	pay taxes	How do I pay taxes?
own	How do I own?	not own	How do I deal with not owning?
assets	How do I handle my assets?	debt	How do I deal with debt?
being rich	How do I relate to being wealthy?	being poor	How do I relate to being poor?

Table 4: Central actions in the area of money and their fragrances

It is a good practice to be aware of just how much our financial actions and thoughts about money influence our mental states on a daily basis. How much energy do we dedicate to money matters compared to other areas in our lives? How much time do we spend thinking about our financial future? What are the financial worries, expectations, and hopes that keep our minds occupied? Do we regret missed opportunities and losses that happened in the past? Are we feeding the wholesome or unwholesome?

True Generosity

Buddhist practice begins with the training of generosity. Generosity softens our ego-centeredness and connects us with our surroundings.

The power of true generosity, meaning giving without the expectation of getting something in return, is highly underrated in today's economy. Many economists view the human being as someone who always counts on personal gain as a return for their actions, even if this benefit might not be immediately obvious.

Generosity (*dana paramita*) is considered one of the highest perfections in Buddhism. Generosity is the ability to give wholeheartedly without any calculation or ulterior motives. The following famous Zen story exemplifies this:

A rich man visited a Zen master. He wanted to give him 100,000 gold coins for a new meditation hall. The man was let in to see the master and heaved the heavy sack with coins onto the floor. He looked at the master expectantly.

Then he said: "Don't you want to count it?" The master didn't answer. The rich man insisted: "100,000 gold coins is a lot of money!" The master still didn't say anything. After a few minutes of silence the Zen monk answered: "Would you like me to thank you? I believe you should thank me."

The story turns our expectations of dealing with money and gifts upside down. We don't always need to seek opportunities to make a profit. We can look for occasions to give, to present someone with a gift and be of help to others. Generous giving brings happiness. This doesn't mean we should give away our livelihood and all we own. It is simply a suggestion to overcome the fear that we and our family might not survive if we care and act selflessly. We shouldn't act irresponsibly, but should look for all the different opportunities in our day-to-day life that allow us to practice generosity.

Berlin city train, January 2009. After a refreshing morning meditation, I am on my way into the city to work. My heart feels wide open and I smile at everyone I meet. It is wonderful. I share my good mood with everyone who comes close to me. During the course of the morning, more than a dozen people smile back at me. Bus drivers start chatting with me, the barista at Starbucks has a wide smile on her face, and the two old women at the bus stop start joking with me. Today I feel connected to all humans, even those who ignore my smile. I keep smiling, feeling that no smile is ever lost.

It is not only our smile or our good mood that we can give away freely. We can also give our time, our joy, our peace, our presence, our freedom, and our experiences. Shunryu Suzuki radically frames it this way: "To give is nonattachment; that is, just not to attach to anything is to give." [11]

Our giving can become freer and freer over time. When giving is truly free, it is no longer attached to any expectations.

> *Berlin, January 2009. My laptop was stolen; my backup was incomplete. Suddenly I have a profound insight. All of the files, images, and documents that I shared with others can be retrieved. Everything I haven't shared is lost. Whatever we give away, we truly own. And what we hold on to will be lost.*

The cultivation and practice of giving freely and without intention to receive something counters egocentric actions. It also breaks with the image of the calculating human held by economists.

Illustration 11, below, clearly shows the different scenarios givers and takers may inhabit. A giver can be someone who gives a gift, who does a favor for someone, or who gives something away, be it of material or immaterial value. The matrix examines the effect of expectations in the process of giving. Expectations may not be present (a), might be present and conscious (b), or might be present and unconscious (c). This holds true for the giver as well as the taker. This results in nine ideal-typical cases.

In case A, two people without any expectations meet and touch the connective joy of dana paramita. In case E, two calculating people meet and make a clear-cut deal. In case I, the actors are both unconscious of their motivation and the result is an unconscious entanglement. The other scenarios showcase all the various misunderstandings that can arise in the field of giving and taking.

---

11. Shunryu Suzuki, *Zen Mind, Beginner's Mind* (Boulder, CO: Shambhala, 2010).

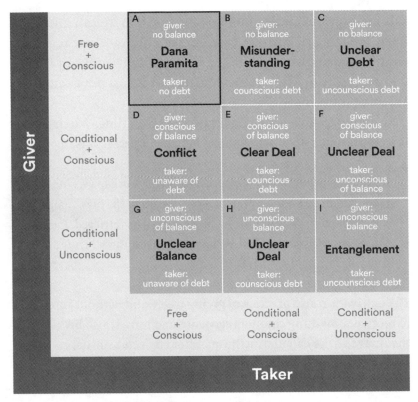

Illustration 11: Relationships in exchange processes

Even a mundane gesture like a greeting or a smile can come with expectations attached. If there is no reaction to our "gift," we quickly react angrily, or are irritated or disappointed. Yet we can work on freeing our gifts from these attachments step-by-step. As we become more aware of our expectations, we learn to smile at them in a relaxed manner and let them pass by more easily.

What Is the Fragrance of Our Possessions?

Our possessions also have a specific scent. We can look at our house, our car, and our everyday items. Are they serving life or simply ourselves? Are they bringing us closer to our environment, or do they separate us from our surroundings? When I used to take walks along Lake Geneva, in Switzerland, I often wondered about the properties right at the water, or adjacent to the lake. So many mansions with full views of the water, boat docks, carefully trimmed hedges and rose bushes. Most of the houses, however, were uninhabited. Very few people lived in these beautiful places. There was so much space that could be shared, so much unused potential. At many of the most beautiful spots in the world we find these empty, unoccupied homes. For me they are a symbol of a missed opportunity to share wealth. It is a symbol of an unwholesome way of handling property.

Properties want to be used. Property that is shared can create connections. Yet in the nature of property lies the idea of separation, the right to exclusivity.

From an economic perspective, if twenty tenants live in a house, and each one of them owns a power drill, that doesn't make sense. If all parties had good relationships with each other, one power drill would be sufficient. Property reduces our dependence on other people, but it might also nourish unwholesome, divisive mental states. The more space that envy, jealousy, greed, arrogance, and fear occupy in our minds, the more we desire exclusivity in the form of property. In our own house, we are free to do what we like. In a way, property protects us from having to deal with other people. When things are shared in a community, our emotional triggers are easily pushed. We need to make compromises, share, and be confronted with ourselves and others. Property provides a buffer for these conflicts.

It is wonderful when property is generously shared. When members of the royalty opened their pleasure gardens and parks to the public in the past, these exclusive places became joyful and lively. We also might carry closed parks and unshared treasures within. Are there possessions we could share, yet want to keep to ourselves? It could be a vacation home on the Baltic sea, a motorhome, or simply our experiences that we could gift another person with. It pays off to bring life into our empty houses.

Do Possessions Define Us?

Ten people may own the same car, but there can be a huge difference as to what degree they each identify with that car. The more we define ourselves through our possessions and derive emotions like pride, joy, security, and recognition from them, the more power we give objects over our life.

Identification is often experienced as love. I love my car; I can't live without my car. I would do everything for my car. The truth is that this kind of relationship has nothing to do with love at all.

When we try to own another person in a relationship and identify with them too strongly, we cause many problems for both our partners and ourselves. Jealousy, worries, anger, and fear will become more present in the relationship.

Financial Success

Financial success can delude us. It is important to see financial success in connection with its origination. As long as we are mindful, we see clearly how we and others earned their money. There are many roads to financial success. Tobacco companies and drug companies, for instance, can be very financially successful, but their successes are based on the exploitation of addiction and destructive actions.

In many other cases it is not so easy to understand the basis of financial success. The financial success of a person may render us blind to the true scent of their success. When financial success isn't based on right livelihood or systematically violates ethical guidelines, it generates collective negative energy.

When I worked as a management consultant, I repeatedly had to make decisions between financial success and my own beliefs. When I chose the money in this kind of situation, and ignored my convictions, I had to pay a high inner price. While our mind is quick in coming up with arguments to support the decision, our heart fights it.

But if our income has a pleasant fragrance, it will touch all areas of our lives. When we happily share with our children how we earn our money, we are sowing wholesome seeds.

The True Nature of Money

What Is My Relationship to Money?

Pick up a pencil and take fifteen minutes to fill in the gaps below on the subject of money. Please don't think too much—try to complete the sentences spontaneously. If you don't notice an impulse to answer, simply move on to the next line.

Money is_____.

I have_____ money.

Without money_____.

With a lot of money _____.

With money, life is_____.

Without money, life is_____.

Money and spirituality are like_____.

My financial situation is_____.

My parents think my way of handling money_____.

Poverty for me is_____.

Wealth for me is_____.

Luxury for me is_____.

My money has the following effect in the world:_____
_____.

_____percent of return is sufficient.

We receive interest for _____.

Working voluntarily is_____.

My money goes to_____.

I receive my money from_____.

For a simple and healthy life you need_____dollars per month.

In order to be content, I need_____dollars per month.

Money is an expression of_____.

In our society, money replaces_____.

Money serves as_____.

The dark side of money is_____.

My inheritance means_____to me.

Property is_____.

The price of a product is an expression of_____.

When dealing with money, I am especially happy when_____

_____.

When dealing with money, I am especially nervous when _____

_____.

If I had ten million dollars, I would_____

_____.

Please put the book aside now, and watch your emotions mindfully. Focus on your breath and give yourself two or three minutes. Now look at the text again. Are there any surprises? Which of the statements do you feel sure about, and which ones do you doubt? Which topics bring up emotions? What makes you happy, and what makes you uneasy? Set the exercise aside. You have gained some insight into the complexity of the subject of money. You might look at the list again in a few weeks and examine your assessment.

Can Money Really Do Anything?

Money plays so many roles. It serves in asset preservation, and as a medium of exchange. It transports energy from point A to point B. It serves to acquire, exchange, and estimate the value of objects and services. Money stores energy and provides flexibility. Money also plays many psychological roles. Money is an expression of trust into the economic order. It signals esteem, status, and power. Money is a shapeshifter.

We should try to understand this phenomenon that shapes our society so strongly, and we should especially try to understand our own beliefs regarding the subject.

In the first part of this chapter, we will examine the central myths in the field of finance, which we will then challenge and question with the help of Buddhist insights. In the second part, we will examine how to bring transparency to our finances.

Myths about Money and Finances

What is the true nature of money? In times like these, it may be appropriate to look at the subject from a fresh perspective. Money is a myth. It is deeply misunderstood and mysterious. Money is a promise, a wide surface for our projections. Let's look at some of the central convictions and concepts in the monetary economy.

Myth: "Time Is Money"

"Time is not money, time is life." This statement by Thich Nhat Hanh appears in every one of the titles of my seminars on money. The preoccupation with money and its pursuit are such a prominent priority in our society. Fifteen years ago, news from the stock exchange was a side note. Today it occupies a much greater part of our public consciousness.

You might be familiar with the term *opportunity cost*. These are costs that arise because an opportunity to make more money is not taken advantage of. If I leave the office now when I could work for two more hours at a rate of thirty dollars per hour, the opportunity cost is sixty dollars. If I clean my own bathroom instead of paying eight dollars per hour to a cleaner, the opportunity cost per hour is twenty-two dollars (this is assuming that I could be working instead of cleaning the bathroom). I can calculate these costs through my whole life. Following this logic, we could even put a price tag on spending an evening at home with our family.

"Time is money" finds its most extreme expression in investment banks and hedge funds. Many of these entities try to generate the highest amount of money in the shortest period of time. Extremely short-term thinking allows investors to lever the existing money by taking out large loans. There are also many financial instruments in high finance that support investors in gaining stable profits over a longer investment horizon.

The projections of future earnings for many companies are often bumped up to push up the share price. This increases the pressure to show returns, which leads to enormous pressure on employees in companies to work harder and longer hours.

In this type of environment, many people feel that they don't have time anymore. Life rushes past them. The myth that time is money separates us from life. Mindfulness helps us to stay in the present moment instead of losing ourselves in the future.

Myth: Wealth Is Independent of Poverty

Material wealth and material poverty are interrelated. Wealth comes from disparities in the distribution of material goods. Wealth is a material imbalance. We read in the Tao Te Ching:

The way of the Dao is heavenly,

It is to supplement the deprived at the expense of the excessive.

The way of the people is different,

It is to profit the excessive at the expense of the deprived.

Extreme accumulation is not part of human nature. It is a human-made concept. When we approve of great differences, or personally aspire to establish these differences, we can bring discord in social or political relationships. If we develop mindfulness and compassion, we gradually return to a naturalness, to a kind of heaven. Our tendency to want to own things decreases.

We might feel that if we don't belong to the upper class, this myth doesn't apply to us. Yet the average Western consumer uses much more than their share of the earth's resources in comparison to the rest of the world.

Myth: Property

There is hardly an idea that comes as naturally to us as that of property and private ownership. During the course of our conversations, we constantly use words like *mine, yours,* or *theirs.* Our language and thinking are steeped in the idea of property. We talk about our children, our house, our dog, but also about our coworkers, our ideas, and our success.

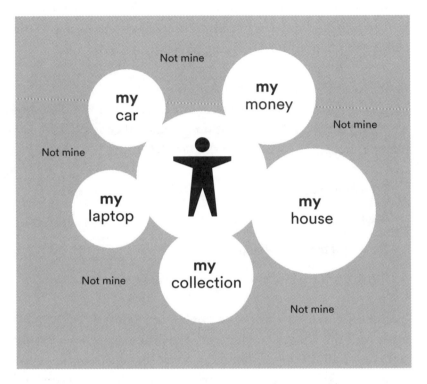

Illustration 12: Some dangerous identifications—illusory property

It seems normal to us that some people own very little or almost nothing, while others own inconceivable amounts. Property seems to be a private matter—it is legally protected, and the owner has rights of disposal and rights of use.

We should understand that this way of handling things is nothing but an idea. It is a concept legitimized only by its usefulness in helping people to simplify or better their relations. There is no divine or absolute idea of property beyond what we have decided it is. When we sit in an airplane, we can see from above that there is no natural separation between things. Clouds move across the borders between nations, atoms and molecules are in constant exchange with each other. On the deepest level, everything is interbeing, connected with everyone and everything else. The idea of property is an intellectual agreement that needs to be accepted collectively or enforced by power.

What really belongs to me? I read this piece of farmer's wisdom posted on the wall of post office in Krems, along the Danube River:

This house is mine yet it isn't mine.

It won't belong to the second one either.

Then the third one will get it.

The fourth one won't live forever.

The fifth one will be carried out as well.

Therefore I ask: Who does the house belong to?

What we call our property today, we might lose tomorrow. The time frame in which we can freely dispose of our accumulated goods ends, at the latest, with our death. Our property will dissipate sooner or later, no matter how clearly the directions in our will spell out our wishes.

Property nourishes our sense that we are in charge of things. If I own something, I can do whatever I want with it. For my personal life and happiness, it is not essential what kind of commodities surround me. It is important, however, what kind of relationship I have to these things.

Myth: Profit

Our society admires winners and champions. We study their success strategies, and young people see them as role models. Buddhist teachers, however, ask us to study the concept of loss.

Studying loss? This piece of Buddhism didn't make sense to me for a long time. "Studying loss" sounds negative, life-negating, and depressing. Why should loss be so important? Shouldn't we focus on possible gains? Isn't it gain that gifts us with positive experiences? Doesn't gain equal success? Shouldn't we avoid losses?

The following story from the life of the famous psychotherapist C.G. Jung helped me understand the importance of the experience of loss. A successful young man visited Jung from time to time. The young man talked about his recent successes. He had married; a healthy child had been born. He had been promoted at work, and his superior predicted a bright future for him professionally. Everything was going very well. When the young man finished, C.G. Jung sighed, turned to him, and said compassionately: "I am so deeply sorry for you." The young man was a serial winner. Yet we learn far less from our victories than from our defeats. Triumphs and successes may mislead us and separate us from what is truly important.

Every human being has to face great losses at some point. We will lose our health, our youth, and finally our lives. We will have to say good-bye to everyone and everything we hold dear today. There is no way to avoid this.

Grappling with loss helps us mature. We are forced to deal with the imperfections in our lives. I gained my most important insights during times of personal defeat. I began to see how my success had cut me off from internal and external realities.

Profit and loss are mutually dependent. They are inextricably connected. If we seek out one side exclusively and avoid the other, we enter a war against reality.

Sharon Salzberg, a well-known Buddhist meditation teacher, writes:

The defeated lose power, freedom, possessions, family and some-times their life. And the winners of the battle are left with feelings of hatred, fear, and envy of those who they conquered. In the cycle of revenge, it is only a matter of time before winners will turn into

*losers. If the struggle of who is better, worse, happier, needier rages
in our own minds, we turn ourselves into losers."*[12]

Our pursuit of winning is in fundamental opposition to Buddhist
and Taoist thinking. The Tao Te Ching advises: "Thus, one gains
by losing and loses by gaining." We win when we let things go. The
Tao Te Ching continues: "Give up ingenuity, renounce profit, and
bandits and thieves will disappear."

This is the opposite of profit maximization. It is a dangerous life
strategy to reap profit from an advantageous opportunity regardless of the losses others might incur. The highest gain can only be
assessed on the spiritual level. Are we now wiser, more content, more
compassionate? Winners who ignore the losers pay a considerable
inner price. We can't live at the expense of others without harming
ourselves. Our true nature is interbeing.

Understanding Our Finances

Hardly any economic sector is as non-transparent as the financial
market. The financial crisis of 2008 showed how misguided even the
most famous and highest-paid financial experts can be. Within the
last several decades, banks and insurance companies have created
a flood of products that only very few people understand. This is a
failure of the industry. Yet it is also a failure on the part of all those
who are clients of these financial institutions. We are the economy.
Therefore, we should try to understand our financial situation more
deeply and comprehensively. We need greater transparency in the
following areas:

- our earnings and expenses
- our current financial portfolio
- financial products we own or are interested in
- how our financial providers are using our money

---

12. Sharon Salzberg, *Lovingkindness* (Boulder, CO: Shambhala, 2008).

Transparency of Earnings and Expenses

How much do I make? How much do I spend?

It sounds simple, but our mindful dealing with money and finances begins with a clear understanding of our own income and expenses. As long as we are unclear about our current financial situation, we have no foundation on which to base our decisions. Many people have only a vague idea of how much they spend. Their spending situation is a black box whose contents remain a mystery. They don't understand where their money has gone at the end of the month.

A first step could be a simple account book or an Excel spreadsheet. When we write down all our expenses for two months, we can gain comprehensive insight into our spending. The actual listing of the expenses itself can act as a mindfulness bell. Instead of spending money automatically, we pause for a moment. We keep an eye on our spending.

Keeping tabs on household expenses on an ongoing basis seems too time-consuming for many people. This approach, however, gives us maximum transparency. Debt counselors report that many people ran into financial trouble because they kept all their receipts in a box and had no clear idea of their spending habits until it was too late.

Transparency of Our Current Financial Portfolio

What do I actually own?

In addition to ongoing earnings and expenses, many of us own assets and property and have debt. Here we also need clarity and a deep understanding of the nature of the asset values, mortgages, and loans. Many banking products are so complicated that only a few experts understand them. Therefore it is not only possible, but likely, that your portfolio also holds assets that are difficult to understand. You might have listened to your financial adviser and now are stuck with investments and securities that you would rather get rid of.

Don't expect that your financial adviser will be your best guide.

Financial advisers represent the interests of their employers and are motivated by personal incentive structures and premiums, which are often not disclosed to clients.

For the purpose of dealing with money mindfully, the following steps are crucial:

- understanding our own portfolio (terms, notice periods, termination consequences, current market values)

- clarification and formulation of our financial plans, needs, and perspectives

- clarification and formulation of our financial motivation (goals versus rate of return)

- definition of a target portfolio that we personally understand or that is recommended by trustworthy experts

- identification of a trustworthy financial partner who shares our values

Transparency of Financial Products

What is this all about? Do I understand my financial portfolio?

Most of us can follow the logic of checking accounts and savings bonds, but it is harder to comprehend other forms of investing, like an option contract. As soon as we start talking about structured financial products,[13] most of us feel overwhelmed. The notorious CDOs (collateralized debt obligations) that wreaked such havoc in 2008 were understood by very few experts, yet many people traded and sold them.

We really should understand our bank products as much as possible. We should understand their mechanisms, their underlying assumptions, their risks, and their spirit. We should only invest in

---

13. A structured financial product is an investment product that combines several basic products, one or more of which is a derivative.

businesses that we understand, truly support, and whose interme-
diaries we trust.

We trust our financial advisers and our banks. We trust them in
the same way we trust the surgeon who will operate on us, and the
computer expert who configures our laptop. We have more reason
to doubt our trust in the financial industry, however. We need to
demand higher transparency.

Our financial markets would be structured very differently if
investors stayed with the products they understood. Our financial
markets have become unstable and volatile for the following reasons:

- Many market participants have no connection to their
  investments. They largely don't care how they make
  their money.

- There are many speculators working in the system who are
  paid by investors for their "services" but don't make any real
  economic contributions.

- Many investors have no patience and think in the short term.

- Expected returns are high and risk tolerance is low.

- The usefulness of an investment is determined exclusively
  by financial measures.

We shouldn't invest in things we don't really understand, or in
products that finance harmful processes. We can ask questions
and demand transparency about the financial products we
are offered.

Transparency of the Financial Product Seller
Who stands to profit? Who is behind the product? What is their
motivation?

Money does not act in isolation. Money is energy. Every dollar is a vote on the kind of economy that we want to support. The energy of money can be used for a variety of purposes. When we entrust our money to the bank, we give energy to that bank and support its purposes and objectives.

We should know our bank and our financial experts well. If we don't know them, we should try to get to know them better. When is the time for a new beginning, if not now? What is the motivation of our bank? What does it offer to its clients? Is the bank's return on equity its most important goal?

Almost all banks continue to rate their products according to interest or return rate promises. It is still unusual to promote non-financial goals as a bank. But it is due to us as customers. We demand high interest rates. We change banks when a new one advertises free checking accounts. But we don't inquire about the dimension of meaning regarding our investments. Are we willing to pay a fee for objective and profit-unrelated consultations? We might not move millions, but our responsibility as small investors is important, and we ought to value it.

Many people are self-conscious when they deal with their banks. As investors and customers we need to get over our fear, paralysis, and lethargy so we can ask the right questions.

There are people in the finance industry with this kind of attitude. We just need to look for them, and we will find them. Ultimately, we are the ones who shape the banks. It is important to bring light and transparency into the banking industry. Our collective willingness to look away has allowed financial institutions to do whatever they want with our money.

Transparency of Purpose

What does my money do? How does it operate in the world? Do we understand how the interest on our bank statement is calculated? Do we know the effects our money has in the world?

When the energy of money doesn't create meaning in the real economy, something is going wrong. We can each make our small contribution by knowing more precisely what our money is doing and by financing well-organized, comprehensible, and meaningful projects.

Beyond the Logic of Banking: The Grameen Bank

In 2006, the Grameen Bank in Bangladesh and its founder, Mohammad Yunus, received the Nobel Peace Prize. The Nobel Peace Prize? For founding a bank? Since then, Mohammad Yunus has been a shining example for keeping our money out of non-transparent, harmful, or pointless circumstances. Yunus bases his work on meaning and trust. He believes in the great potential of the poorest people in his country and tackles concrete problems in his projects. In many cases, he does exactly the opposite of what he observed traditional banks do in his home country when lending funds:

- micro-loans instead of huge loans

- loans for the poor instead of the rich

- trust instead of securities

- no credit checks

- loans for women instead of men

- obligation toward borrowers instead of shareholders

- dividends that include useful payment in kind instead of solely money

- focus on the community instead of the individual

- success means improving the life circumstances of the borrower, as opposed to purely financial returns

- bankers visit the client as opposed to clients visit
  the banker

For a long time, other bankers thought Yunus was crazy. Yet his success proved them wrong. Grameen loans improved the situation of the poorest people and especially of women in Bangladesh. Since its inception in 1983, the bank has offered loans to eight million borrowers, according to its own reports. Entrepreneurial freedom created a new class of small business owners in Bangladesh, with repayment rates of 98 percent, which are significantly higher than those of consumer credit in Western countries. Yunus once said that all he had to do in order to be sustainably successful was the opposite of what was accepted as normal in the banking sector in Bangladesh.

When we clearly define the purposes of our money and have it work toward meaningful goals, like Yunus did, our way of dealing with money changes dramatically. We become interested in the effects of our money in the world. We can reclaim the energy of our money and funnel it into more wholesome projects.

What to Invest in?

The dominant mode of economic thinking currently takes every area in our society and analyzes it from the perspective of profitability. Everything from pig stomachs, to private elementary schools, Finnish wood, and nuclear power plants is a possible way to make a profit. When we look at the world through the eyes of a profit-oriented investor, all we see are streams of proceeds and disbursements. We need more investors with direct relationships to their objects of investment.

Our economy should help us to do and realize meaningful things. An economy without meaning is nothing but a restlessly spinning machine trying to perpetuate itself.

Financial Blossoms

When we understand the true nature of our money, we become mature investors, savers, and consumers. We will no longer ignore what we do with our money and what purpose it serves. We also gain confidence in assessing the central actors in the finance system and questioning their principles and projects. A seminar participant said the following:

> *For a long time, I felt foggy and fearful when the topic of money came up. I handed over my responsibility to the so-called experts. In the end, the money was gone and so was the expert. I learned my lesson. It is up to me to look into investment possibilities, to find out what I want to support. There are so many great ideas which only need a small amount of money to blossom. That's the direction of my money's future.*

Financial Balance

The Dangers of Affluence

We live in a society that values accumulation, the constant acquisition of "more" in all aspects of life. A period of no growth is seen as a setback. We assume that we need "more" in order to be happy. It is harder to figure out what exactly this "more" might be, however.

Most spiritual traditions agree that the pursuit of wealth and riches is one of the greatest obstacles on the way to higher human development. What is appropriate for us? What is the right balance? Where does excessiveness begin?

It is easy to succumb to the temptation of aiming "higher, farther, and faster." Yet we humans are limited beings. Humankind needs to maintain a balance to allow our long-term survival in harmony with all other beings on this planet. Excessiveness can destroy us. We can ask ourselves the following questions:

- How do I know when it is enough?

- How do I define financial normality for myself?

- What are my financial entitlements based on?

- How much do I own compared to others?

- What are my financial expectations?

- How do I handle my assets?

- Do I share my wealth with others?

- How do I deal with financial restrictions?

First, we will address some problems associated with excess, and then show how the cultivation of patience, gratitude, letting go, and simplicity can help us to find our personal balance and move toward financial freedom.

The Problem of Excessiveness

Eleven years ago I read a book written by Bodo Schaefer titled *The Road to Financial Freedom: The First Million*. The book caught me in a phase when I was searching for new paths in my life without an inner compass or mental clarity. Why shouldn't I strive to become a millionaire, I thought. The more I read, the more I felt I didn't have enough, and the greedier I became.

When we have an arbitrary financial goal for ourselves, like becoming a millionaire, we can run into several problems. We don't know whether we will reach the life we desire, and if we don't, we might see our life as a failure. And even if we do accomplish our goal, we can't be sure we won't lose our wealth again, leading to a cycle of fear and attachment.

Holding On: The Acquired Strategy of Wastefulness

When we collect possessions, we hold on to things. A bicycle becomes my bicycle. No one is allowed to use the bicycle without my permission. When we hold on to things, they can no longer freely serve their purpose. Here is an everyday example:

> *Berlin-Schöneberg, January 2008. I am at the swimming pool with my son. On the upper floor of the city pool there is a saltwater pool, two whirlpool baths, a twenty-five-meter swimming lane, and around thirty-five chairs. All the chairs are empty. There are no human bodies resting here. Yet there are bags, towels, and robes sitting on every single one of them. This is the poverty of holding on. It is the poverty of non-sharing or claiming for oneself.*

The more we own, the more things belong to us, the harder it is to use every single object in our possession. We can't wear two pairs of shoes at the same time. If we make a list of all our possessions and their utilization rate, we will find a number of things that we never use. The degree of use for German cars is approximately 4 percent. The rest of the time, the cars sit around idle. Yet it is hard for us to share our cars. We want to keep the individual, exclusive right of use as our personal freedom.

Skewed Comparisons

Measuring anything is always a comparison. Who are we comparing ourselves to? Where do we get our financial benchmarks and entitlements? Do they come from our family of origin, from our friends, from the society we live in? What is financial normalcy for us?

When we compare our financial standards only with the living circumstances of our friends and our neighborhood, we are actively disengaging from other living worlds. We need an absolute measure that we can use independently from societal norms and benchmarks. Without a universal measure, our standards will fluctuate depending on our environment.

We need to distinguish between a simple life and material hardship. Material hardship exists when a human's basic needs are not met:

- food and water
- shelter
- health care
- clothing

When these four dimensions are covered, we have fulfilled our basic human needs.

For many of us, our current material situation far exceeds these minimal standards. I am not suggesting that we should return to these minimal standards and give up our current prosperity. The question is whether or not we could imagine a happy life with just our basic needs fulfilled. Are we afraid we could plummet into this kind of "poverty"? Do we imagine a life on social welfare as a life in hell?

The Buddha laid out clear rules regarding property and money for his monks and nuns: every ordained monastic was allowed to own three robes, a water filter, a begging bowl, and small everyday items, like a toothpick. Living without possessions sent a clear signal to the rest of the world that they encountered: that we do not need money and property to live a happy life. Merchants, politicians, and tradespeople were offered the chance to consider a different path to happiness when they met the wandering monks and nuns. The monks and nuns lived a life independent of money, power, and societal status.

How to Train Our Sense of Proportion
Scrooge McDuck, Donald Duck's uncle, is worth one multiplujillion, nine obsquatumatillion, six hundred twenty-three dollars and sixty-two cents. Even when we aren't talking about silly exaggerations, we have great difficulty imagining numbers with several zeroes, once

they go beyond an annual income or the price of a single family home. For two decades, I have made it a habit to check high numbers I see in the media for plausibility. It is surprising how often even reputable media outlets get these wrong by several zeroes. Billions become millions, and billions become trillions. Many of us don't have a natural sense for big numbers, and so those kinds of mistakes aren't easily caught.

This is a problem. We need a sense for these numbers in order to understand the current processes of the financial markets. Without a sense for these numbers, we cannot have a deeper understanding for worldwide markets. We need to be able to experience numbers in relation to our lives; otherwise they remain abstract and aren't on our radar. Let's try the following experiment. Try to assign prices of items, projects, and other financial processes to the numbers listed below. For example: $1 = a pair of scissors, $1,000 = a new laptop, $100,000,000,000 = bailout package for Hypo Real Estate, and so on.

$1	$10,000,000
$10	$100,000,000
$100	$1,000,000,000
$1,000	$10,000,000,000
$10,000	$100,000,000,000
$100,000	$1,000,000,000,000
$1,000,000	$10,000,000,000,000

Although we may never have to deal with amounts of money well above a cost of a home or our annual income, we should be fluent in these numbers, as well as what they might correspond to. Doing so helps us be more informed consumers within the global financial system.

Balancing Four Criteria

As long as we are not in poverty, our material situation has only a limited influence on our happiness. Richard Layard, a British economist and professor at the London School of Economics, has demonstrated this phenomenon in many studies and publications.[14]

The concept of real "having" is slowly losing its significance. Much more significant is the relation between "having" and "wanting." Our wanting depends on how much we compare ourselves with our neighbors, friends, colleagues, family members, or other people. I am unhappy when I wish for more than what I already have. When I have more than I wish for or than I need, I can relax and live contentedly.

We can differentiate four criteria or dimensions:

What we have: "This is what I have at my disposal at this time."

What we want to have: "This is what I strive for."

What I spend: "This is what I currently spend."

What we have mastered: "This is my realistic financial potential."

What I have is a combination of my income, my assets, and my debt.

What I want to have combines my wishes, my entitlements, my plans, my personal expectations, and the expectations of my environment.

My spending is influenced by my lifestyle, my obligations, and my diligence when handling money.

---

14. See, for example, Richard Layard, *Happiness* (New York: Penguin, 2005).

My mastery has to do with my income possibilities, my learning capacity and willingness to learn, my education, the current labor market, my market value, and my contacts.

A > B	B. wanting	B. having	B. consume	B. mastery
A. wanting		unhappiness	moderation	excessive demands on yourself
A. having	happiness		saving	income vulnerability
A. spending	wastefulness, unconsciousness	debt		lifestyle doesn't match qualifications
A. mastery	understatement, under one's potential	earning potential	lifestyle meets qualifications	

Table 5: Relations among wanting, having, consuming and mastery

The relationship among these four criteria is decisive for the assessment of our financial situation.

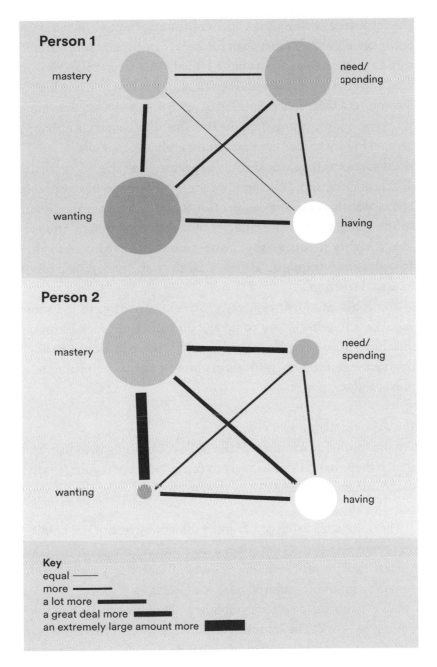

Illustration 13: Analysis of the four criteria

The income of person 1 matches her income potential. But she currently spends more money than she has at her disposal, and wants to spend a considerable amount more. If this behavior continues, she will acquire debt. The only way to compensate the debt would be a higher income. Yet a higher income is out of reach unless she acquires more skills and qualifications. Despite overspending, she feels unhappy because her wishes are even greater than what she spends.

Person 2 has the same income as person 1, yet she is in a totally different situation. She spends a lot less than she has available and is able to put money aside. Her wishes are rather moderate, so she is happy with the current situation. In addition, she forgoes a higher income—she hasn't maxed out her market value according to her qualifications. Therefore she has quite a bit of financial freedom.

You could draw out your own financial situation in the same way. As a fifth criteria, you could add the minimum social support (disability or unemployment benefits) that you would receive in an emergency. This minimum amount can be helpful to take into account.

The Joy of Letting Go

Try the following exercise. Make both your hands into fists and clench them hard. Count slowly to thirty. Now open your fists, let the inside of your hands show upward, and let go of the tension. How does this feel?

The process of letting go, of setting something free, of not holding on, of non-attachment describes a deep and central process of our human life. This process happens every minute, many times within ourselves: grabbing, holding on, letting go. ...

It is exhausting to keep on grabbing and holding on. Yet how does "letting go" work? The Buddhist meditation teacher Reb Anderson advises us to not force the process of letting go, but to concentrate on the object that we hold on to. When we realize the problems we create by holding on to an opinion, a thought, an object, or something else, the insight and the wish to let go of this state will arise. This kind of mind training is designed to make our mind more malleable.

Our society is based on holding on. It is hardly surprising, then, that the subject of "fighting" is ever-present in day-to-day life and in the media. The mode of "fighting" is the natural strategy when there is a difference of opinion or a conflict of interest. We fight for majorities, jobs, about our children, for world peace, and—time and time again—about money.

Mastering the process of letting go requires a lot of practice. There are several tried-and-true methods in Buddhism.

Here are the five remembrances, a widely practiced meditation, which helps us to become more familiar with letting go.[15]

1. I am of the nature to grow old.
There is no way to escape growing old.

2. I am of the nature to have ill health.
There is no way to escape ill health.

3. I am of the nature to die.
There is no way to escape death.

4. All that is dear to me and everyone I love are
of the nature to change.
There is no way to escape being separated from them.

5. My actions are my only true belongings.
I cannot escape the consequences of my actions.
My actions are the ground upon which I stand.

---

15. Thich Nhat Hanh, *Chanting from the Heart* (Berkeley, CA: Parallax Press, 2002).

Many illnesses of our time might be healed if we learned to make do with less. Sacrifice and letting go can create new spaces for us.

Balanced Spending Card

The Buddha advised his lay students to handle their money consciously and mindfully. There were many entrepreneurs among his students who spent their wealth for the common good of the community. The Buddha advised them to keep four areas in mind when dealing with money:

- one's own livelihood
- savings for old age
- support of one's own family
- support of the society

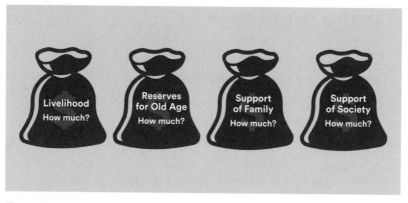

Illustration 14: Financial areas of activity

Many people will regard these four areas as an impossible task, only attainable by the wealthy. They are happy when they can manage to support their own livelihood or their family's. Yet the more money we have at our disposal, the more we can pick and choose. We need to find the right balance. Reflect on your own finances to see how you balance the four areas. How are you doing?

Overcoming the Fear of Having Less

The fear of falling below one's standard of living is widespread, especially in the middle classes. After World War II, material wealth increased steadily for most people. Today, however, times are much more insecure. Almost everyone can lose their job at any time, and the fear of unemployment paralyzes us. Deep down in our collective consciousness there is a conviction: "The more you have, the more you are."

During my long stay in the monastery, I lost my fear of material decline for the most part, and my ideas about wealth and poverty changed. I know that I can be happy with extremely little money, as long as I keep working on my mental development and live with like-minded people. Living at the bottom rung of the ladder doesn't scare me that much anymore.

An anonymous voice on the internet expressed my experience this way: "Social poverty is when no one smiles back, when the smile freezes in your face."

Self-restraint

Our society is oriented toward growth. We are always looking for new things we can get, rather than what we actually need.

There is a story by Leo Tolstoy, written in 1886, called "How Much Land Does a Man Need?" that I've found instructive. It tells the story of the peasant Pachom. After Pachom buys his first piece of land, he becomes possessive of it and is eager to acquire more property. This causes arguments with his neighbors, and there are rumors of arson. He moves away to the east, where land is affordable and fertile. He builds a small fortune. There are, however, always richer neighbors, and he gets into fights with them. So he moves farther east, where the Bashkirs live in the endless expanse of the steppe. They don't have a concept of owning land. They are willing to sell land to Pachom for a very low price. They will sell him as large an area as he can walk between daybreak and sunset. Pachom overestimates his endurance, and returns too late. As the sun is setting, he runs to the point of exhaustion, and collapses as he reaches the Bashkirs. He is dead. His servant buries him in an ordinary grave.

It is much more beneficial to focus on one's own needs instead of striving for an external ideal. Do I really need this? How will this promotion affect other areas in my life? A graduate of a top economic school said to me: "As soon as you are offered the starting salary of a business consultant, all the other offers seem pathetic." We have to find a way to deal with these temptations.

Self-restraint is an essential key to financial and personal freedom. I can disconnect from the collective consciousness and define for myself how much I need. I can refuse to compare any longer. In the Tao Te Ching, it says: "Therefore he who knows that enough is enough will always have enough." And I would add: whoever doesn't know that enough is enough will always experience a life of want.

Mindful Handling of Debt

Fundamentally, debt is neither good nor bad. Money and debt are generated concurrently in our modern economy. Economic activity always creates and requires temporary imbalances. Money must flow. Money is a promise of payment by banks to the money owners. Debt is a promise of payment to a private or an institutional creditor.

Debts cause few problems as long as borrower and creditor:

- agree on reasonable terms

- make sure that they have and keep good relations

- make all risks transparent

All too often, the true cost of debt isn't transparent. There are many hidden fees that must be taken into consideration. Debts are seductive. They heighten our energy in the present and lower our energy for the future. They establish long-term commitments and obligations. We should know whom we trust. If we look carefully at our debt, we will see whether our finances are balanced. We will also see the motivation that led us to incur debt, and we can change that motivation.

If our debt has become too much, we shouldn't avoid thinking about it. We can reconfigure our debt and possessions, and settle for a more realistic debt that won't make us feel imprisoned. We can also try to improve the quality of the relationship to our creditors. In an extreme case, a reconfiguration might require us to go through private bankruptcy. A new beginning is always an option.

Waiving Returns and Interest

The principle of self-restraint is helpful when we apply it to our finances, especially when dealing with investments. The lower our expectation of return, the more we can relax. If we quit the race toward the highest rate of return, we find ourselves sailing much more smoothly. A participant in a money seminar told me:

> We didn't have a lot of money when I was growing up. During the last few years, however, I saved quite a bit, developed an interest in the stock market, and bought stock. I have also meditated on a regular basis over the last ten years, so I was able to observe the mental effect my investments had caused. In the past, I never thought much about money. I had lived in a monastery for a long time. Now I noticed how my thoughts often drifted toward my stocks during the day. I worried and followed the share prices. My hunting fever gripped me. It was surprising how much agitation entered my life. When I noticed that, I sold all of my stocks, and I'm sleeping much better.

If we are wealthy and abandon the idea of wealth preservation, we can invest our money without any return pressure, according to criteria we choose ourselves and that are meaningful to us. If we free ourselves of the classic concept of maximizing returns, our worldview broadens. We discover the beauty and joy of using our money meaningfully instead of focusing on wealth preservation and securing our current standard of living into old age.

Letting Go of Entitlements and Expectations

When I assert a claim, I am convinced that I am entitled to something. The House of Wittelsbach believes to be entitled to Salem Castle. We believe that we are entitled to good service, a good education, a salary increase, or a specific rate of return on investments.

We can make demands, insist on them, and fight for them. As soon as we believe, however, that we are objectively entitled to something, we are deluding ourselves. We should be honest with ourselves. Entitlements are never objective or right; they are self-centered and narrow by nature.

From a Buddhist point of view, entitlement is a great source of suffering. Freedom lies beyond demands and expectations. This freedom is available to everyone. When we meet people who let go of their expectations, we can feel their radiance and freedom. They radiate true love and humanity. They don't ask us for anything, and they are fearless. Many spiritual leaders walked this path. Gandhi, Buddha, Jesus, Nelson Mandela, and many others let go of all demands in the desert, in prison, or by conscious fasting and restraint. They realized that the freedom from expectation could be very powerful.

Touching Abundance and Cultivating Gratefulness

Take a piece of paper. Make a list of everything that is missing in your life. What do you wish for? What do you need to have? What should change? When you are done, make a second list of everything that supports, nourishes, and sustains your current life: people, living conditions, objects. Take your time. This list should be at least twice as long as the first one. When you think that you are done, close your eyes, and think about everything that happened last week. Maybe you have something else to add now.

I received this exercise ten years ago, with a group of many others, from Thich Nhat Hanh. When we were done, he added that we could easily cross out more than half of all our supporting factors and we would still have more than enough conditions to live happily. We so easily ignore the fact that we have so much. When we have a toothache, we wish for nothing more but for the toothache to stop. When we don't have a toothache, however, we forget that we are in this wonderful condition of not having a toothache. Without mindfulness, we miss out on what we already have and run toward something that is apparently missing. A Zen poem that my wife loves says the following: "A mountain of gold would not be enough to repay all the love the universe has given to you."

When we touch on the logic and experience of abundance, we can leave the mental game of not having enough. We realize that we have more than enough already.

The Ideal of the Simple Life

Our lives have become very complicated. All over society, people are wanting more simplicity. Usually, our lives get a lot simpler when we reduce our possessions. Most people whom I accompanied on their paths of mindfulness practice reach a point when they want to give away or sell things they no longer use. They develop the need to cast off any unnecessary ballast.

Many of humanity's greatest teachers lived a very simple life. They had few possessions and owned almost nothing. They dressed in simple and functional clothes. They fasted and concentrated on the essential. Buddha didn't eat more than one meal a day and walked through all of India. Gandhi lived like an Indian peasant, made his clothes himself, and was silent for a whole day every week. Jesus retreated into the desert to meditate.

True simplicity is the result of focused training of the mind. When we learn to see things as they are without assigning superfluous meaning to them, our thoughts, words, and actions gain clarity. This will affect our relationship with money and our possessions.

We can exchange the house that is now too big for a smaller apartment, and make room in our closets and basements. An uncluttered environment has an effect on the mind. And a clear mind wants an uncluttered environment. As our life gets simpler, we get more use of our possessions. Instead of twenty shirts, we own ten. We save a lot of money without losing any quality of life. These concepts are true economics. We know what we need and we actually use what we own. We don't acquire useless items that require attention and care. A simpler life has many beneficial dimensions and is of great importance for a mindful economy.

The Joy of Owning Less

We are all familiar with the joy of owning something or receiving a gift. Every possession, however, has its drawbacks. We need to pay the mortgage for the house. A new shirt needs to be taken to the dry cleaner, and the dog needs exercise and regular visits to the vet. A large inheritance can be a burden and keep us very busy.

Rumi, the famous Sufi master, once walked through the weekly market in his hometown. He had a wide smile on his face. A friend asked him why he was in such a good mood. He answered with a laugh: "I enjoy looking at all the wonderful things that I don't need."

Twenty years ago, I bought a black VW beetle. It was a real lemon. It looked great on the outside, but the interior was a disaster. I had to bother my father, who had warned me not to buy the car, to come and pick me up on a regular basis. I put a large part of my money into this car, and I had to pay for its maintenance. I was happy when I could finally sell it. Since then, I don't own a car anymore. A lot of the work and the problems that keep car owners busy don't occupy any space in my life. I don't pay for car insurance, I don't get speeding tickets, I don't cause accidents, I don't worry about rising gas prices, I don't fear vandalism, I don't need to look for parking, I don't spend time in traffic, I don't pay for inspections, and much more. At the same time, however, our family has to do without the advantages of a car. Every decision not to own something results in advantages and disadvantages.

Community Creates Space

Community structures are disappearing. In many large cities, more than 50 percent of all people live in single-person households. When we leave the safety net of community, either by choice or unintentionally, our day-to-day social relationships can turn into financial relationships. Without extended family and a tightly knit neighborhood, there are fewer connections to rely on and fewer duties to share. When grandparents can't watch the children, we need to hire a babysitter. If we don't know our neighbors, we need to replace neighborly assistance with purchases. We replace mutual and free support with paid services.

My wife lived for five years in a Buddhist monastery community. I lived there for two years. We learned a lot about the limits of an individualized lifestyle. Life in vital communities with integrity has many advantages, and not only financial ones.

When we moved to Berlin and lived in our small household of three, we couldn't believe how expensive it was to live as a small family. It seemed absurd to us to use a washing machine for only three of us and spend a lot of money on babysitters. When we looked at the financial side of things, living in larger communities has unbeatable advantages. We need far fewer resources compared to living alone or in single family housing. Living in a community makes the most sense economically. Again we run into the paradox that the solution that is most economical for an individual (resource sharing, mutual support instead of additional purchase of services) is deemed catastrophic for overall economic development.

Who is going to buy all the beautiful washing machines if we are

sharing them? How can we do this to our economy? What about
the jobs in the industry? It is an economical joke that we ask these
questions. Should we act antisocially to help our economy function?
Isn't it the ultimate joke that our efficient economy encourages
us daily to be wasteful? Without wastefulness, this very economy
couldn't exist to its current degree.

There would be no need for the lion's share of today's products
if we conducted ourselves more mindfully and oriented ourselves
toward the experiences and precepts of this book. Imagine that the
world economy shrank by 50 percent over the long term. Unimag-
inable? Fatal? If it happened all of a sudden—maybe. The end of
civilization? I don't think so. Over the long term, our civilization is
certainly more threatened by excessive growth and consumerism
rather than conscious fasting. What would happen if we used fewer
goods and still had enough to fulfill our true needs? Wouldn't that
be wonderful?

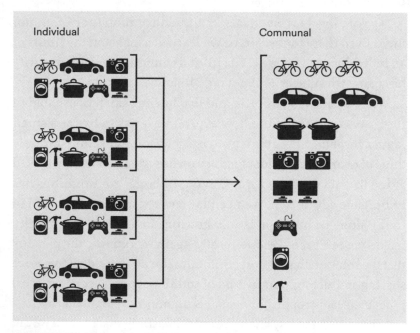

Illustration 15: The economics of community

Would the reduction of consumption be so bad? We aren't meant to consume mindlessly. We are the economy! The economy is here for us, not vice versa.

Many economic actors are afraid of this kind of frugality. Our politicians boost the economy in the short term by taking on billions of debt at the expense of future generations.

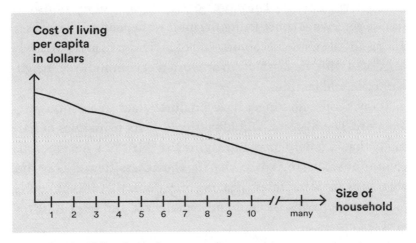

Illustration 16: Riding down the community curve

You may have heard of the concept "economies of scale." These are the cost advantages that companies obtain when they increase their level of production and gain greater experience in the production process—"riding down the experience curve." Interestingly enough, we practice the exact opposite as a society: our households become smaller while our cost of living per capita increases. From an economic perspective, the individual lifestyle is the most expensive. In production theory we talk about lot size one—a custom-made product.

A community can be seen as an anti-consumer. In a community, many services are exchanged without a price or a market. The ideal consumer is an individual without a community. When there is no community, we have to turn to the market. Whoever has no handyman in the family needs to hire someone and pay them. When there are no children who like to help out when the parents are older, we need to hire someone or live in a retirement home. When we don't know our neighbors, we need to run to the store when we need one more egg to make spaghetti carbonara. The individual promotes the market economy.

The farther we step away from a living community, the more we need to rely on money. The more we free ourselves of relationships that we perceive as constricting, the more we depend on the market. The rise of the market economy and of individualism is positively correlated with the dissolution or erosion of communities, neighborhoods, and families.

Many people no longer have a natural place in a community anymore. The historical Buddha provided six principles of harmony that can help us to reimagine the spirit of a harmonious community: sharing space, sharing the necessities of daily life, abiding by the same rules, speaking only words that are conducive to harmony, sharing insights and experiences, and respecting the views of others.

The six principles of harmony can be learned with a lot of practice. It feels like a miracle when we get to know communities that make an effort to live by these guidelines of unity. There are many dysfunctional communities: authoritarian extended families, ideological groups, sects, and others. Many people really have a deep longing for living with others and collaborating together. Every one of us has experienced moments when we touch this positive community life. Instead of fostering more individualism, we could focus more on functioning, happy, and peaceful communities.

Experiment: A Day without Money

The most important things in life are free. We might have heard that before, but do we believe it? If we believed this as a collective, we wouldn't live the way we do. But we can give it a try by living a day without money.

We can start by making a list of all the activities that we enjoy that don't cost anything. We can also ask our family and our friends what they do for fun that doesn't require money. We add their answers to our list.

We may explore offers in our hometown that are free of charge. We may also collect ideas about places nearby that we can bike to. If it is fall, we could go out looking for wild apple or pear trees; we could go hunting for mushrooms. We take our time making the list, so it will get longer. Then we pick a day in our calendar: a day on which we won't spend any money. We might spend it alone or together with friends. The only thing not allowed is spending money. A day like that might let us get in touch with the joys of a simple life. It might show us that we can live a happy and fulfilled life without a lot of money.

The Motivation of Money

Money's Siren Calls and Promises

Money offers many promises. We can't really examine these promises for ourselves, as only a few among us will ever own great riches in their lives. It seems reasonable, then, to learn from those who came into a lot of money and share their experiences openly. Aside from the Buddha's life story, I was especially impressed by the story of Bhaddiya:

Bhaddiya accompanied Buddha. He had been a powerful governor of an Indian province before his ordination as a monk (Bhikkhu). Now he lived a modest life as a monk and slept under the trees outside at night. One night Bhaddiya sat in quiet meditation, and all of a sudden he shouted: "Oh, what endless bliss! Oh, what endless bliss!" Another monk heard this. He had been worried that Bhaddiya would miss his wealth and fame. He went to the

Buddha and told him about the exclamation. The Buddha gathered Bhaddiya and the whole community around himself. He asked Bhaddiya whether he had actually called out, "Oh, what endless bliss!" two times during the night, and what this was all about. Bhaddiya answered: "Master, when I was governor, I lived a life full of fame, power, and prosperity. Wherever I went four soldiers accompanied me for protection. My palace was watched by armed guards night and day. And there was never a moment when I felt safe. I was always full of fear and restlessness. Now I can walk and sit on my own in the deepest forest. I don't know fear and anxiety anymore. I feel peace, joy, and a sense of well-being that I've never known before. Beloved teacher, it makes me so happy and brings me such great contentment to lead the life of a Bhikkhu. I don't live in fear of anyone else any longer, and I'm not afraid that someone will steal from me. I am as happy as the deer that freely roam the woods. Last night during meditation I realized all this, and so I exclaimed: "Oh, what endless bliss! Oh, what endless bliss!" Please forgive me this disruption that I have caused for you and the other monks.

Many wealthy students of the Buddha left their titles, businesses, and possessions behind to walk the path of developing the mind and truly helping other people.

As long as we lack inner clarity and direction, all the money in the world won't help us. Money is an energy that may either support us or burn us. In this chapter we will ask the following questions:

- What do we expect from money?

- What and who do I support financially?

- Am I really familiar with my financial habits?

- What are my patterns in dealing with money?

- What drives me?

- What standards do I set?

We start with an examination of our desires.

Who Wants to Be a Millionaire?

The game show *Who Wants to Be a Millionaire?* has had the highest rankings on German TV for a long time. Millions of people cheer on the players and dream of hitting it big themselves. They dream the dream of winning big money. What are their expectations? How realistic is it that this dream won't lead down the wrong track? Why do millions of people buy lottery tickets every time the jackpot rises?

During my youth, millions of Germans were fascinated by the American series *Dallas* and *Dynasty*. The American dream played out in our living rooms as we followed the lives of oil millionaires with nearly unlimited financial possibilities, power, luxury, and sexual escapades. The fascination with this lifestyle prevailed, even though the downsides of life in financial and material abundance were displayed as well.

Why is money so attractive to us? And why do spiritual leaders warn us about its dangers? We have seen which emotions can be attached to money. We have also seen how impatience accelerates the flow of money, fear makes us hoard money, and that money can have very beneficial effects when used with compassion.

The true power that money plays in our life only becomes accessible when we understand our deepest motivations clearly. Here, it is worthwhile to examine some interdependencies that aren't obvious at first glance. We hope that money can solve or alleviate the underlying problems in our lives. We assume and hope that money can fill a void in our lives or allow us to hold on to something in the long term. As human beings, we want to be happy and develop convictions and strategies to that end. Money is a central key in this matter.

Our Deepest Aspirations: Searching for Happiness

Let's leave money aside for a moment and look at our deepest needs. Let's ask ourselves what kind of life we are looking for on a non-material level. Do we want security and recognition? Do we long for friendship and community? Every human being has his or her own hierarchy of immaterial wishes. Yet we all have one thing in common: we want to be happy as human beings. Let's begin with our wish for happiness.

Happiness is a large concept. Every person understands it differently. Books about happiness have been in high demand for a long time. An exceptional book about happiness was written by the French monk Matthieu Ricard. He is a trusted friend of the Dalai Lama, has a doctorate in molecular biology, and has fascinating discussions with brain researchers like Wolf Singer and others. He describes how we all wish for happiness, yet we know very little about the true nature of happiness. Ricard quotes a Tibetan proverb: "Seeking happiness outside ourselves is like waiting for sunshine in a cave facing north." Ricard continues:

> We go to school for a dozen years, and then we spend several more years at a university or in professional training. We go to fitness centers to stay healthy, and we spend a lot of time increasing our comfort, our own prosperity, and our social status. We invest so much energy in these things, yet we do so little to improve our inner conditions, which are essential factors of the quality of our lives. What strange indecisiveness, fear, or indifference keeps us from understanding the true essence of joy and sorrow? What keeps us from truly looking within? [16]

Ricard's analysis is unambiguous: we are professionals in many areas, yet when faced with the subject of happiness, we are amateurs. We cling to the old promises of "how to reach happiness" that we

---

16. Matthieu Ricard, *Happiness* (New York: Little Brown, 2008).

were given in childhood. We mistake happiness for excitement or restless anticipation. We believe we experience happiness when we are merely able to take an opportunity to relax.

In order to experience true happiness, we need a deep familiarity with the condition itself. Training of the mind is necessary. Otherwise, how would we know whether we are on the right path to happiness? How do we know whether our life is happier? It is essential to understand our mind, a knowledge we only acquire through training, so that we don't fall for a superficial idea of happiness. Moshé Feldenkrais summarized the importance of this knowledge for our decisions in the following sentence: "You cannot know what you want to do until you know what you do."

Meditation teachers keep emphasizing that the greatest happiness is unconditional happiness. It is a type of happiness that doesn't depend on external conditions. This happiness comes about when we rest deeply within ourselves and are able to connect with everything that is.

If this is true, money cannot be a key to happiness.

The Five Promises of Happiness
So many promises are made that supposedly lead us to happiness—as if happiness can be some kind of arrival at a certain place or state. The Buddha makes us aware that we should examine these promises carefully to avoid arriving at a dead end. The following promises about happiness are especially prevalent:

- Power brings us happiness.

- Fame brings us happiness.

- Wealth brings us happiness.

- Sensual pleasure brings us happiness.

- Sex brings us happiness.

These five beliefs are deeply ingrained in our public consciousness. They lead to fascination with celebrities (fame), politicians (power), models (sex), billionaires (wealth), and seductive things, experiences, and foods of all different kinds (sensual pleasures). If we are not careful, we will easily be hooked by these five attractions.

Money: The Great Shapeshifter

What is the special feature of money? Money gives us access to these five areas of human existence. Money is the great shapeshifter. Money can buy power, fame, sex, and sensual pleasure to a certain degree, or ease the access to these spheres.

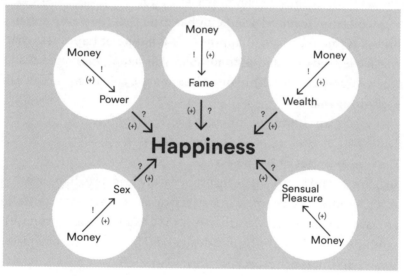

Illustration 17: Five spheres of shifting

Money and fame: Billionaires are often famous and celebrated for their wealth alone. Money facilitates access to celebrities and allows us to participate in events that ordinary citizens could never attend. The rich can become sponsors or investors and subsequently increase their own prominence.

Money and power: With money we hold power, because money is an energy that works for us, and we can make it work for our goals. When we pay others to work for us, we increase our own strength and our influence. Money also facilitates access to politics. Creditors can become dependent on us. Gifts create dependencies. We can buy advertising time, place ads, and hire lobbyists to advance our interests. Money also allows us to exercise control over goods and services.

Money and sex: Money attracts. Wealthy people are more likely to find sexual partners.

Money and wealth: With money it is easy to gain access to more money. The rich often remain among themselves. There is the saying: "The first million is the hardest." Experience shows that it gets easier at a certain level to multiply one's money. The wealthy receive better and more exclusive information, they can afford better advisers and staff, and they have access to borrowed capital and business contacts. With more money, we can take greater risks and make more profits in the long run.

Money and sensual pleasure: With money we have easy access to all sorts of sensual pleasures. Wine, food, hotels, travel, ayurvedic massage—the possibilities of sensual pleasures are unlimited. The more money we have, the more unusual and exquisite pleasures are available.

So Does Money Provide Happiness?
So it must be true, after all: money does make us happy, because it allows us to enjoy all these wonderful things. Thich Nhat Hanh and many generations of other Buddhist teachers don't think so, however. Their experiences are different.

Sensual pleasures create the illusion of happiness but in actual fact they are a source of suffering. A healthy human stays away from the flames of sensual craving. The source of true happiness is living in ease and freedom, fully experiencing the wonders of life. Happiness is being aware of what is going on in the present moment, free from both clinging and aversion. A happy person cherishes the wonders taking place in the present moment—a cool breeze, the morning sky, a golden flower, a violet bamboo tree, the smile of a child. A happy person can appreciate these things without being bound by them....Because one understands that a flower will wilt, one is not sad when it does.[17]

We play a dangerous game when we tie our happiness to power, fame, riches, sensual pleasures, and sex. We become subject to endless desires that will never completely fulfill us. We will feel great disillusionment and uncertainty when we realize that we have spent so much time and energy on the wrong path. A dream that is fulfilled and turns out to be an illusion is actually worse than a dream that does not come true.

Let's take another close look to see whether money:

• brings us security and control

• gives us comfort

• provides us self-esteem, respect, and recognition

• increases freedom and independence

• brings us happiness

Playing It Safe

Money is closely connected with the concept of security. We try to protect ourselves financially. We buy insurance and keep savings

---

17. Thich Nhat Hanh, *Old Path White Clouds* (Berkeley, CA: Parallax Press, 1987).

accounts. Money can give us the feeling that we are more in control of our lives. The feeling of control calms our fears. It is deceptively calming, however. Our fears will not simply disappear when we pack them in cotton wool. Just the opposite happens: when we ignore our fears, they control us subconsciously.

Berlin, 2007. A seminar participant tells me that during the retreat he began to understand why he had collected twelve expensive suits in his closet. When he worked as an independent coach with difficult groups, the suits served as a protective shield. He felt self-confident and professional. He had a protective shield of exquisite new wool. He realized that the true motivation for the purchase was his fear of failure and the hope to gain a feeling of greater security. A year later, he told me that he started sitting and breathing with his fear. He felt great relief and no longer depended on his suits.

Fears lose their power over us only when we observe them mindfully and confront them head-on. The reality is that we can't control our life and it is never secure. We have no control over our body, our family, our thoughts, our reputation, the moment of our death, our health, or our finances—not even over the next five minutes. Our human life depends on innumerous interactions that are not controllable. Life is fragile, vulnerable, and manifests itself anew in every moment. This is the realization of mindfulness practice.

Money doesn't provide us with deeper security. Fame acquired with money will pass. Even with wealth, we must helplessly watch those we love die. Money won't give us the refuge we seek.

There are more appropriate strategies to use if we want to feel secure or nurture fearlessness. There are ways that help us overcome our fear of impermanence, death, and illness, ways which let us touch our true nature. We can gain some security when we familiarize ourselves more and more with impermanence, constant change, and the interdependence of our existence.

Money and Deceptive Comfort

We wish for a comfortable life and assume that money can help us achieve it. Here is an exercise. Study the following list of projects and activities. Consider which of these you would most like to do and which you would least like to do. Number the activities from 1 (the most) to 20 (the least).

fill out tax return	install software	repair bike	exercise
paint apartment	send out invites	read textbook	clean out basement
clean apartment	go out for a meal	attend a party	take away recycling
vacation in Bali	book tickets	play with children	meet friends
make lunch	buy gifts	pay bills	meditate

Did you sort the list?

Money allows us to delegate a number of unpleasant or time-consuming tasks. Money can take care of what we consider tedious, laborious, and boring. We hire babysitters, and we call someone to pick up the broken bike. This is how our list could look after we eliminate the tasks we don't like:

vacation in Bali	~~buy gifts~~
meet friends	~~book tickets~~
meditate	~~install software~~
exercise	~~pay bills~~
play with children	~~take away recycling~~
go out for a meal	~~clean apartment~~
attend a party	~~fill out tax return~~
~~send out invites~~	~~clean out basement~~
read textbooks	~~repair bike~~
~~make lunch~~	~~paint apartment~~

Money creates a comfort zone for us. It allows us to increase what we consider pleasurable and to avoid what we consider unpleasant. Many people believe this is ideal. We can be on permanent vacation. We give up the job we don't like. Life is sweet: we meet friends, see movies, enjoy lattes. We use our money to reduce our contact with the unpleasant.

The Comfort Trap

Unfortunately, increasing our comfort zone doesn't hold in the long run. By having others perform many daily tasks for us, we continuously shrink the range of duties that we are willing to take on. The more preferences we have, the more effort we expend on organizing, and our comfort zone decreases. The more differentiated our needs are, the harder they are to fulfill.

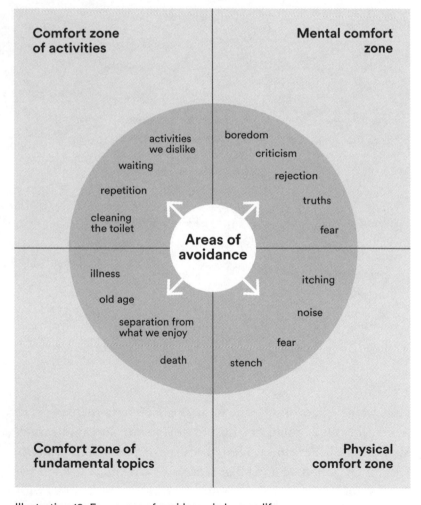

Illustration 18: Four areas of avoidance in human life

What we perceive as unpleasant has many different faces and shapes. We want to avoid it. We undergo tremendous physical, mental, and financial efforts to escape from it. After we make a lot of money, we can avoid performing undesirable activities. No more cleaning toilets or washing shirts and windows. We take painkillers to avoid feeling our pain. We turn on the TV so that we don't experience the nagging feeling of boredom or loneliness inside us. We try so hard to avoid anything unpleasant, yet we cannot escape it. It follows us like a shadow.

The person who feels at ease everywhere enjoys the greatest comfort zone. They do not need to run when something unpleasant happens. They accept the unpleasant and smile at it. Shunryu Suzuki writes: "For Zen students, a weed, for which most people is useless, is a treasure."[18]

With the help of money, we can remove weeds from our life temporarily. If we do practice with weeds, however, we confront the unpleasant. This gives us the opportunity to overcome our resistances instead of letting our moods and preferences govern us.

When we practice, we learn to reconcile our life little by little with all different kinds of people, situations, and strokes of fate.

The Result of Non-acceptance: Anger and Irritability

Let's examine another part of ourselves: our anger, our rage, and our aggression. And the weaker relatives of anger: irritability, resentment, and displeasure. All these mental states come from the same source. We notice something we don't want. We reject it. We want the world to be different. Couldn't it be friendlier, more supportive, more appreciative? We want the world to change. Shouldn't it provide for us exactly what we wish for?

When we are angry, we can't see the world clearly. Anger places ourselves into the center of all events. Anger makes us vulnerable

---

18. Shunryu Suzuki, *Zen Mind, Beginner's Mind* (Boulder, CO: Shambhala, 2010).

for wrong perceptions and judgments. Anger can lead to hatred, and hatred is the origin of all ideologies. Ideologies are compost for the roots of war. When we learn to tame our anger and our wrath, we become true peace workers. Anger and resentment prevent meaningful cooperation. If we harbor resentment, we deny even the most reasonable cooperation for the good of all, whether in politics, in the market, or in our private lives.

There is a small everyday anger that arises when we want to avoid something we deem unpleasant or when we fear that we will lose something we like. Yet something very small already harbors the big. Something big has its roots in something small. Aggressive corporate strategies and business policies harm all of us. If we don't guard our negative words and thoughts, we may poison our relationships, our workplaces, and our communities. How much energy is wasted every day by harassment at work? How much creativity do we lose through aggressive behavior? It is difficult to work in an atmosphere of separation and fear.

Money and Self-esteem

In many circles, money is seen as a status symbol. Money assigns a measurable and comparable value to our activities. How much do you earn per hour? What is your daily rate? Where do we stand in comparison to others, to our neighbors, to our school friends? Money is recognition. Money is praise. Money gives us the feeling that we have achieved something valuable. A management consultant I worked with put it this way: "Money for me is an expression of respect. It is a recognition of my work and my achievement."

Money can also give us the feeling that we have accomplished something. We completed a project or performed a service, and we are rewarded with money or other means. This provides us with security and the feeling of belonging. Yet this feeling of security is only borrowed. It cannot replace our underlying hunger for true community and deep security.

Can Money Grant Us Freedom?

Financial independence and financial freedom sound like music to our ears. But freedom is a larger and often misunderstood concept. In economic contexts, freedom is usually seen as the opportunity to increase or maximize personal options. I can buy myself whatever I want, and I can use my assets in whichever way I please. Entrepreneurial freedom means that economic activities are minimally regulated and left to the market.

In the broader sense, we understand freedom as an unimpeded and protected opportunity to do something: freedom of speech, freedom to travel, freedom of choice, freedom of religion, freedom of movement, and more. We are free to do many things.

In Buddhism, the concept of freedom has a different origin. Liberation is the ideal. We aspire to gain freedom from our inner fetters instead of the freedom to do or not do something in the outer world.

A famous meditation about compassion says: "May we be free of attachment and rejection without becoming indifferent."

We are not so much concerned with external freedom as with internal freedom. The Dalai Lama asks us insistently: "Do you possess the insight that leads to spiritual freedom?" Without this insight, all the financial options in the whole world won't help us. Chögyam Trungpa says:

> Freedom is generally thought of as the ability to achieve goals and satisfy desires. But what are the sources of these goals and desires? If they arise from ignorance, habitual patterns, and negative emotions—psychologically destructive elements that truly enslave us—is the freedom to pursue these goals true freedom, or is it just a myth? [19]

---

19. Chögyam Trungpa, *The Myth Of Freedom and The Way of Meditation* (Boulder, CO: Shambala, 1988).

Buddhist meditation aims to liberate the mind from delusion and wrong perception. The liberation of the mind leads to non-attachment to material things and other objects of perception. Meditation liberates us gradually from bad habits, wrong perceptions, and the dominance of unwholesome states of mind. We let go of unnecessary worries and regrets.

What a comprehensive concept of freedom! We become familiar with our negative, positive, and neutral mental formations through continuous meditation. We learn to accept them, to embrace them, and change them. We can let go of the seeds of rage, fear, and pride, seeds that our ancestors and our society passed on and nourished in us. What is it that we want to let go of, or should let go of? How do we imprison ourselves inside. What are our addictions?

The freedom to choose promised by a full bank account seems rather modest compared to this spiritual freedom.

Do Not Maximize Your Options!
Our economic system suggests that personal freedom is connected to the expansion of opportunities for personal agency. The more choices we have, the freer we are. Maximize your options! Keep as many doors open as possible! For a different conception of freedom, we can look to Immanuel Kant. For Kant, freedom is not found in maximizing options, but in the free, conscious, and mindful choice of limits and restrictions. I choose a certain standard of living, I choose a profession and a life partner. Freedom exists in the fact that we make meaningful decisions and walk and remain committed to this path through thick and thin.

A person who has run out of choices due to earlier decisions in a particular situation may have in fact reached ultimate freedom. Free decisions in the past brought the person to this point, rather than the limited options of the current moment. Freedom here is not understood as a right, but as a commitment.

Money that Serves a Cause

In the novela *A Christmas Carol,* by Charles Dickens, the mean-spirited and heartless businessman Ebeneezer Scrooge experiences a surprising transformation. When confronted with his own death, he realizes the consequences of his selfish deeds and suffers a healthy shock. He begins to open his heart, share his fortune, and experiences a never-before-known love and joy.

Money can be used to experience the joy of helping as well as the joy of meaningful activities. Money should flow and support meaningful projects. Members of the Order of Interbeing in the tradition of Thich Nhat Hanh follow Fourteen Mindfulness Trainings. The fifth training says:

> Aware that true happiness is rooted in peace, solidity, freedom, and compassion, we are determined not to accumulate wealth while millions are hungry and dying nor to take as the aim of our life fame, power, wealth, or sensual pleasure, which can bring much suffering and despair. We will practice looking deeply into how we nourish our body and mind with edible foods, sense impressions, volition, and consciousness. We are committed not to gamble or to use alcohol, drugs, or any other products that bring toxins into our own and the collective body and consciousness, such as certain websites, electronic games, music, TV programs, films, magazines, books, and conversations. We will consume in a way that preserves compassion, well-being, and joy in our bodies and consciousness and in the collective body and consciousness of our families, our society, and the earth.

When we touch the spirit behind these words, it will become increasingly unnatural to us to use our money only for us, within our close circles, or to invest it in solely profit-oriented products. We gain a much wider financial perspective when we cultivate the spirit of loving kindness and compassion.

The joy of giving and taking part in meaningful change seems more important to me than legal obligations and paying additional taxes for high incomes and assets. When we do our part in connecting our money with meaningful causes on an individual as well as a collective level, we will change our economy radically. We will withdraw energy from unwholesome processes and contribute to wholesome processes with our money.

We Are the Consumers

We are a people of consumers and customers. Every one of us is a part of product cycles, value creation, and purchase processes. Consumption is the acquisition or usage of material goods and services. We consume bread, ice cream, and gas, but also employ babysitters, get haircuts, and buy insurance policies. In a general sense, consumption is a central economic variable that shows what and how much of any particular commodity is in demand.

We need to distinguish between physical (material) and mental (spiritual) consumption. Material consumption means that we take in physical objects (food, beverages, and other products) into our body or into our household. When we consume mentally, we absorb thoughts, ideas, theories, or sensual perceptions (sounds, forms, smells, touch, or taste).

Buddhist psychology stresses that spiritual consumption has a strong effect on the quality of our life. Whatever we allow to penetrate our mind, and how we handle what we consume, shapes our days. When we consume too much discontent and anger, we feed the seeds of discontent and anger within. We are the gardeners of our own mind.

Both material and spiritual consumption has risen continually during the last few decades. How do we evaluate this development? Some insist that growing consumption leads to superficial materialism, exploitation, and destruction, while others see consumption as a venue for personal expression, economic freedom, and even a source of well-being. Consumption, the thinking goes, is the indispensable motor that creates new jobs and prosperity.

Dangers of Consumption

Why is consumption so tremendously important? Why do so many people spend their free time in malls? Are we truly awake and aware when we bring all these objects into our lives? What do we expect from consumption? The following developments in the area of consumption are problematic:

- when we consume things that hurt our body and mind

- when we are not really present during the process of consumption and do not make conscious decisions

- when we have unrealistic or unconscious expectations about the objects we consume

- when we consume excessively and cannot find a way of saying "enough"

- when we consume in a way that is not sustainable and endangers our environment

- when we become dependent or fall into addiction

Mindful consumption protects our body and mind and promotes wholesome economic processes. Unmindful consumption may destroy us as individuals, families, and societies. Whatever we consume on a regular basis—whether these are foods, ideas, or movies—will shape and form us.

Four Dimensions of Mindful Consumption

Mindful consumption means that we want to establish a meaningful and lasting relationship with the things we bring into our lives. Before a purchase, we ask ourselves whether we really need this object (being conscious of our purchase decision). When we use the object, we do so consciously and appreciate it (being conscious of usage). And we take conscious leave, when reasons like wear and tear, energy inefficiency, and incompatibility suggest that we should let an object go (being conscious of discarding and recycling).

Consumption is a choice. When we choose, we choose our own future and the future of our society. Our consumer behavior creates buying power. Buying power, in turn, creates new products and new markets. This is the power we own as consumers.

Without mindfulness, we might consume:

- harmful things

- in a harmful manner

- in harmful quantities

- for harmful reasons

Mindful consumption means that:

- We stay alert during the process of consuming and do not submit to unwholesome mental formations (the fragrance and mental quality of my consumer behavior).

- We know what we are consuming, so that we understand the effects that the consumed object or service might have on us and upon our immediate and further environment (the true nature of my consumption)

- We know our interior and exterior balance in regards to how much we are consuming (balance of my consumption).

- We know the motivation of our consumer behavior and won't let ourselves be governed by unwholesome motivations (motivation of my consumption).

We will examine how we can shape these four dimensions of our consumption more mindfully and in a more meaningful way. We will start with the fragrance, the mental impact of our consumption.

The Fragrance of Consumption

How do we consume? Consciously or unconsciously? Are we free or do we feel driven? Responsibly or inconsiderately?

Plum Village, 1999. This is the first day of my meditation retreat. Vegetable casserole is for dinner. I am with approximately one hundred other men in the large dining hall of the monastery. We sit in silence and practice mindful eating. Our instructions seem simple: we want to be aware of every single bite. We are to chew at least thirty times, and we won't let our thoughts distract us from our food. After every bite, we put our forks down. This is very hard for me. My thoughts go in many directions, and I keep eating on autopilot. After ten minutes, my plate is empty. I didn't pay attention for a large part of the meal. The people sitting next to me keep on eating with concentration and in a relaxed manner, while I have to contend with my impatience. It is interesting to become aware of the things happening in my mind while I am eating. After a week of practice, my eating behavior has changed completely.

There is hardly another area that reflects our consumer habits so clearly as our eating behavior. How do we eat? One of the most powerful meditation practices is eating meditation. Give it a try with the instructions mentioned above. Take some time and observe the fragrance of your spirit and your thoughts. All of this is part of our meal, be it joy or impatience, freedom or compulsion. We set our own mental table. Yet emotions are not only tied to food. Every object of our perception is colored by our spirit.

Hunger and desire change the objects in our surroundings, making them more desirable than they really are. It is our state of mind that colors these objects of consumption. How often do we ask ourselves after a spontaneous purchase why we just acquired that item?

How do unwholesome mental states affect our consumer behavior?

Unwholesome mental state	Perceived absence or need	Consumer strategy
Fear	Lack of security	Numbing with alcohol or cigarettes
Jealousy/envy	Another person has what I want for myself.	Emulating status symbols
Grief	Loss	Overeating, consuming too much
Discontent	It is not/never enough.	Closing the gap by consuming, participating in the rat race
Anger	Things don't go my way.	Rewarding ourselves
Greed	I need this; I want this.	Impulse buying, looking for good deals, buying
Inferiority	I am less than others.	Compensation by consuming

Table 6: Unwholesome states of mind and their effect on consumer behavior

We can actively work with the unwholesome mental states mentioned above. We can acknowledge them and gently transform them, even though we would rather just get rid of the feelings. We don't want to feel irritated, angry, or inferior, and we thoughtlessly seek refuge through consumption. It seems like a quick solution. We turn on the TV or we have a beer. We have developed many strategies to suppress or repress the unpleasant. Yet this leads us directly away from freedom.

Advertising professionals, marketing experts, and PR consultants know our weaknesses and desires. They target their products right onto our escape mechanisms. A Tibetan monk who saw the blinking neon signs of New York for the first time reacted: "They are trying to steal our mind."

Mindfulness helps us to stay awake. Only when we are awake can we take precautions not to allow our thoughts and moods to be captured by salespeople and marketing strategists.

The Nourishing Meal

The quality of a meal depends on what we eat and how we eat. It is possible to increase the quality of our food when we eat mindfully. On the other hand, we can buy the best fruit, the healthiest bread, and organic carrots, yet the quality of our meal ultimately depends on our eating behavior, our appreciation for the food, and the mental state we are in while we eat. A seminar participant said the following:

For me, eating was always a waste of time. A tedious burden. While I gobbled up my food, I truly ate my impatience and my anger. Today I eat much more consciously and with more joy. I have a lot more energy.

The way we go about eating an apple plays a significant role in how the apple will nourish us. Mindful eating supports the integration of food into our body. We use the time we spend eating in order to relax and to pause. We don't feed tension and stress during the meal but rather recovery and regeneration.

Mindful eating protects us from taking in harmful things while eating. We nurture gratitude, joy, and concentration instead of restlessness, stress, and anger.

Are We in Control of Matters?

Are we consuming, or are we consumed? Who is consuming whom? When I am on the subway and pick up a newspaper that someone else left behind, I sometimes ask myself, who really decided to read this? When I am tired and unfocused, it almost seems that the newspaper reaches for me and is actually the one forcing me to read. Many objects of consumption develop a similar pull:

- Do we eat chocolate, or does the chocolate grab us?

- Do we listen to the radio, or does the radio insist on our listening?

• Do we look at the ad, or does the ad scream at us?

• Do we think these thoughts, or do they think us?

• Are we actually shopping, or are we coerced to shop?

Without mindfulness, we are no longer in control of our consumer processes. We are guided by our unconscious habits, ideas, and mental states that connect with external objects. We need to steer deliberately toward the cultivation of mindfulness and wakefulness in the consumer process, instead of following internal and external impulses.

Instant Consumption

With access to online shopping, the objects of our desire are often only a mouse click away. Mere seconds pass between the impulse to buy and the actual purchase. We receive a book recommendation by email and order the book thirty seconds later with one click on Amazon. That is very convenient, yet also somewhat dangerous. Before we shopped online, purchases required a lot more effort. The purchase process proceeded in several intervals and between these intervals there were pauses that allowed us to stop and reconsider whether we really needed the item.

At the point of sale, before the retail action is completed, we are bombarded with specials, hot deals, and promotion codes. These create a perceived atmosphere of urgency that doesn't really exist. Many impulse purchases turn out to be superfluous or even annoying after a few days. For this exact reason, sellers generate an atmosphere of urgency during the purchase process. They know that the buyer will be in a completely different mental space by tomorrow. The mental fragrance that led him into the store will have evaporated, and the object of purchase has lost some of its allure, seems too expensive, and not really suitable, even superfluous.

What Sticks to the Product?

Many products today are marketed as more than just the product. A car is not simply a car. The possession of a certain car is an expression of identity for many people. It is an expression of certain values, allegiance to a societal group, a signal of financial strength. Cars include, apart from their material upgrades, many immaterial extras as well. Marketing experts find nothing more boring, threatening, and irritating than a car that is simply a car. They want customers to envision their dream car with all the bells and whistles. They want us to project power, success, intelligence, pride, aggression, environmental awareness, and unconventionality onto the car.

For many branded products, it is the image and not the product itself that is deemed important. Following this logic, the fragrance of a product is more important than the product itself. Companies might spend many times more to lodge a certain image in their customer's brains than on the actual costs of production and raw materials used for a particular product. Within the concept of a mindful economy, these perfumes are superfluous, harmful, and unwholesome. Economic areas that produce and support illusions, false perceptions, wishes, and desires are not useful to us but do waste resources. Many of our products have lost their simplicity.

Impulse Control: The Key to Freedom

In every moment, action impulses arise in our body and mind. An impulse is a trigger urging us to act, either on a physical level or on a mental level. Impulses light up within us before we say, think, feel, or do something. We can easily miss the impulse and act on it right away. As long as we stay unaware of this process, we cannot act freely—we can only react. The higher our reactivity, the lower our freedom. Freedom in this context means not to follow an impulse blindly, but to make one's own decision. If our distance to the impulse is minimal, we are open to manipulation and lose liveliness and clarity.

Impulse distance is the ability to clearly recognize a bodily or mental impulse, to be aware how it rises up and subsides, without having to give in to it. Impulse distance saves us from letting our negative emotions run rampant or act with unwholesome intent. With this distance, we can see the possible consequences of our actions and make a clear-minded decision.

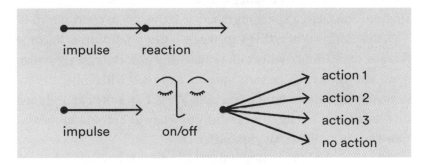

Illustration 19: Essential qualification impulse distance

The following impulses whiz through our minds every day:

- "I really need this."

- "If I only had this, I would be really happy."

- "Just one more time."

- "I should treat myself."

- "I have earned this."

In this situation, it helps to pause and come back to the breath. When we stop, we loosen reactive patterns and become aware of our automatic judging, evaluating, and commenting. We are able to actually think instead of reacting. We pause before we buy something we don't need, before we say something we might regret later, before we stress about unlikely future scenarios. Impulse distance gives us true freedom.

Creating Space Inside

Many areas in our lives can be ruled by impulses: our judgments, our emotions, our communication, and our buying and eating behaviors.

In order to regain freedom, we need the space between impulse and action. Zen master Shunryu Suzuki put it this way: "To give your sheep or cow a large, spacious meadow is the way to control him."[20]

Without this space, this gap, when other possibilities become feasible or desirable, we act like a machine processing a rigid program. We listen to someone's opinion and react with anger. We are nervous and have to light a cigarette. We get into the car and turn on the radio. If we are not careful, our life will become more and more machinelike as we grow older.

Who actually wants to respond like an impulse-reaction machine? If we don't want to go down that path, we have to consciously try to create our freedom.

Watching Impulses Mindfully

Impulse distance does not simply happen. It must be cultivated. We are capable of learning to observe our impulses in both body and mind clearly and distinctly. As we watch an impulse through its entire cycle, it loses its power over us. It arises, grows stronger, weakens, and disappears. Impulses come and go. When we are aware of them, we no longer have to follow them.

An effective impulse arises from the depth of our consciousness, grows stronger, finds its way into our conscious or unconscious perception, causes an action, and sinks back into our store consciousness. During this process, it will be strengthened. An ineffective impulse follows the same cycle, yet it does not cause an action, and returns weakened into our store consciousness. When we give in

20. Shunryu Suzuki, *Zen Mind, Beginner's Mind* (Boulder, CO: Shambhala, 2010).

to scratching an itch, we will have to scratch it more often. When we resist an itch, we have less of an urge to scratch in the long term.

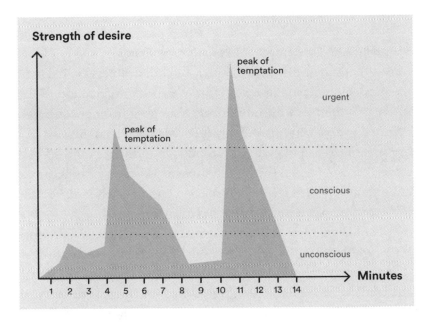

Illustration 20: To buy or not to buy?

A participant in a seminar describes the effect of impulse distance as follows:

During my first meditation seminar, my thinking slowed down quite a bit. When I entered our local shopping center on the following Monday to get a few small items, something unexpected happened. I could clearly notice how my thoughts accelerated. A flood of buying impulses and comments came up. I noticed commands, arguments, and promises. It was unpleasant. I returned to my breath and immediately these voices became quieter and I could relax. Since that day I can no longer take my thoughts that seriously.

When we practice mindfulness, we can notice how our impulse distance is reduced by unwholesome states of mind like anger, greed, and fear.

Shopping with Concentration, Resisting the Extras

At no other time are impulse control and mindfulness as vital as in the moment of a purchase decision. We are exposed to especially intense influences while shopping. Shopping in a concentrated manner is very liberating. We stay focused on our shopping list and our breath instead of giving in to outside influences and special offers. We can practice this in the supermarket every day. It can be enlightening. When we stay alert and conscious while shopping, our consumer spending is often drastically reduced.

It is a delight to decide for or against the purchase of a product if we can do it in a relaxed, conscious, responsible way, according to meaningful criteria. We take our time; we sense and examine our true needs. We don't get carried away by interior or exterior impulses to buy anything. As we buy or do not buy mindfully, we gain insight into why we decide for or against a product. If we can shop in a mindful way, we create a new economy, which will offer meaningful, intelligent, durable, environmentally friendly—and probably also fewer overall—products.

If we understand the true nature of impulses, they lose their power. During sitting meditation, we can experience how a seemingly unbearable impulse to scratch an itch disappears, because we don't give in to it, but rather follow it throughout its whole cycle with a smile. Having witnessed this process, we regain freedom in our lives. It is only through mindful observation that we gain a sense of the influence that arbitrary, unconscious, and often harmful impulses exert on our life, our choices, and our decisions.

Contentment: Virtue or Enemy of Progress?

Contentment serves as the key to inner peace and equanimity. If we let go of the belief that we need more than we have, we can be at peace. Then we can also appreciate and enjoy what we have. Observe this verse from the Tao Te Ching:

There is no greater sin than desire,
no greater curse than discontent,
no greater misfortune than greed.
He who knows that enough is enough,
will always have enough.

Consumption and discontent go hand in hand. Discontent is a dangerous fuel which drives and accelerates the motor of our economy unnecessarily. The higher the discontent, the higher the economic growth. It is a perverse correlation.

Economic players dread contentment and frugality. If these mental states were to spread widely, the utilization of our productivity capacities could be at risk. In this context there is a valuable story from Ajahn Amaro, a Thai monk:

In the late 1950s and 1960s, when Thailand entered the international markets, the Thai government took an extraordinary step. It asked the leading abbots and teachers of the Thai Buddhist community to no longer encourage the virtues of santutthi *(moderation) and* mattaññuta *(knowing the measure in eating) in the country's population. The effort to increase productivity and consumption deemed moderation and happiness as obstacles to the economic program. It is sad that most members of the monastic community gave in to this request. A prominent teacher, however, Ajahn Buddhadasa, wasn't afraid of the ruling powers. Ajahn Buddhadasa showed that greed, selfishness, and wastefulness are harmful qualities. A healthy economy should be founded on wholesome rather than unwholesome principles.*[21]

---

21. Ajahn Amaro, *Hooked: Buddhist Writings on Greed, Desire and the Urge to Consume* (Boulder, CO: Shambhala, 2005).

Is our economy healthy? Is it based on wholesome mental states? Does it become inflamed by discontent? Feeling content is a real danger to many forms of unwholesome consumption. Mindfulness helps us to end these consumer processes and realize that they will not contribute to anything lasting or useful. I do not act intelligently when my consumer behavior feeds my discontent.

We also shouldn't confuse contentment with laziness, idleness, or a lack of motivation. Happy and content people can be very active and driven. Their actions are not guided by a sense of lack, but instead by a sense of inner abundance.

Gratefulness

Our affluence can lull us to sleep and make us ungrateful. It is only when we lose something—a friend, a family member, a job, or a home—that we realize the genuine value of it. Difficult times are excellent teachers in terms of gratefulness. Yet in our everyday routines, we lose our gratefulness for what we already have.

When we receive food when we are hungry, water when we are thirsty, community when we are lonely, or warmth when we are cold, we might wake up again and experience new appreciation for what we take for granted. In times of material abundance, we need to remind ourselves how lucky we are. The Gatha on eating meditation says: "May we eat in such a way that we deserve to receive this gift."

When we eat in the spirit of gratefulness, we inoculate our mind against a sense of entitlement as well as against envy, resentment, jealousy, and greed. These states of mind are mental plagues. Gratefulness will stop us from finding one or two strands of hair in the soup of our lives.

Letting Go of the Entitlement Mind-set

Walking through life with high expectations, wishes, and dreams is a direct route to disappointment and bitterness. We might believe that we should make more money or receive a promotion. We might

crave more recognition or respect. "I have earned this." "I am entitled to this." "I sacrificed so much for this." Our entitlements arise
from our life situation, education, performance, health, marital
status, or current position of power. There is nothing wrong with
asking for certain things—the problem arises when we are convinced
that we are entitled to them. This is the starting point for conflicts,
fights, and wars of all kinds. We lose our gratefulness and humility.
The more expectations we build, the more disappointments we
experience. It all depends on our perspective. If we don't expect
anything, all that we receive is a gift. If our expectations are unrea-
sonably high, we perceive everything that we don't receive as a loss,
an affront, or an injustice.

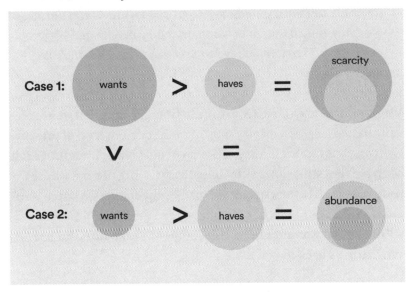

Illustration 21: Relativity of scarcity and abundance

We are all in danger of losing our gratefulness. We take for granted
what we are given on a daily basis and do not see our wealth for what
it is. We are focused on what we do not have. This type of mind-set
will lead to discontent. Gratefulness is the antidote.

Presence in Daily Life

The starting point for mindful consumption lies in making an effort to maintain an elevated level of mindfulness all day long. Those who haven't practiced a lot often overestimate themselves and feel very present and concentrated during their daily routines. The more we practice mindfulness and the higher the level of mindfulness that we reach, the more clearly we recognize how often we get distracted. Tenzin Droelma, a Tibetan Buddhist nun, says:

> Based on honest self-assessment, the participants of my advanced meditation group believe that they are mindful and awake between 5 and 10 percent of their consciously spent time. Practice makes us modest and shows that our mental states during everyday routines aren't characterized by clarity and correct perception. Therefore we need to practice so that we don't keep falling asleep.

We should ask ourselves from time to time how present we are on a daily basis. Imagine a display showing your current level of presence right on your forehead. Are you at 20 percent? Being present at a rate of 20 percent still allows us to live a functioning life, but we are not truly present. The newspaper we read or the movie we watch won't really enrich our lives, but might just feed the unwholesome seeds within us. We should not let this happen. Three mindful breaths can bring us back to real life.

Business Lunch with a Zen Master

During the Vietnam War, Thich Nhat Hanh was invited for a luncheon with several United States Senators. While soup was served, the senators—Robert Kennedy among them—began asking questions. Thich Nhat Hanh answered patiently. When he was done, he turned to the soup, filled his spoon—and in the same moment he was confronted with the next question. Again Thich Nhat Hanh put his spoon aside and answered the question. Then he took up his spoon again and was faced with another question. This went on for twenty minutes. The senators had finished eating, the business lunch was over, and Thich Nhat Hanh's soup was cold and untouched. When he talks about this incident today, he says: "I hate business luncheons. They are not civil."

Yet business lunches have become more and more common. We keep on working while we eat. We also eat while we sit at our computers. This is how we lose contact with our food and with ourselves.

Thich Nhat Hanh asks us: "Are you here for your tea? The tea is here for you. If you aren't here, you will miss the tea. Life happens in the present moment. If you miss the present moment, you miss your life."

When we begin to drink our tea more mindfully, it will have an effect on our whole life. What could be more tragic than a consumer society that doesn't know the art of consuming?

We can create alternatives to business lunches. A friend of mine who works in a large firm met with members of his company meditation group in the staff cafeteria for mindful eating over an extended period of time. We can also leave the cafeteria behind and enjoy our lunch quietly outside in the park.

In my teacher Thich Nhat Hanh's hermitage hangs a calligraphy that reads: "*Bois ton thé!*" The invitation isn't easy: "Drink your tea!" It is the essence of Zen practice. We are asked to drink our tea without adding anything else. If we succeed, we become one with the tea. We are no longer drinking our plans, our worries, or our daydreams.

Whenever we are offered a cup of tea, coffee, or a glass of water between meetings, we can take the opportunity to practice this. We let go of the agenda of the meeting for a few moments and dedicate ourselves completely to enjoying our drink. If we can do this, we will be more awake and refreshed when we return to the meeting.

Protecting Our Senses in Everyday Life

When I returned from a meditation retreat for the first time, I traveled to Hamburg via Paris. In the Paris Metro, I was surprised by how urgently the ads displayed there interacted with my mind. Sensitized to be more aware of my states of mind, I could watch in slow motion how the image of a half-naked woman aroused me, or how the look of a cool-aggressive model irritated me. As I walked through the underground passages I felt that I was perfumed with many different mental states and ideas. I had never recognized this process so clearly—it was terrifying.

When I take the bus home in the dark, the only thing I see besides streetlights and lighted windows in homes are advertisements. I practice to ignore these. I don't want to engage. This is not easy and depends on my daily state of mind. As I walk through the inner city of Berlin, this gets even harder. Advertisements and bright signs are omnipresent. Yet I always try to engage in the practice of non-engagement. I remain focused inward and stay with my breath.

Simple Ingredients for an Extraordinary Feast

When we host a celebration, we often invest a lot of time, energy, and money to make sure that we will have a wonderful evening. Yet there are very few parties that stay with us, making lasting and pleasant memories. Many parties do not really allow the guests to connect with each other. We drink, we eat and talk a lot, yet at the end of the evening we are overcome with a feeling of emptiness and exhaustion.

In my experience, many parties are missing something essential. Two crucial ingredients are missing: mindfulness and awareness. When we mindlessly gobble up a piece of cake, it cannot really satisfy us. And it is the same with an evening we spend with guests who are not truly present. We don't get to know one another.

After I grew to know and understand the practice of mindfulness, my way of celebrating changed radically.

Berlin, January 2008. Retreat of the Network for Mindful Business. After three days of intensive mindfulness practice, seventeen people gather in a circle to celebrate an informal tea ceremony. At the entrance of the meditation room, our team greets the guests with a bow. We appreciate one another, sit down, and begin with the ceremony. After a short while, the tea master fills the tea glasses in a concentrated and reverent way. Then we pass the plates with tea and cookies around. It is a simple exercise. We say thank-you for the tea and also for the cookie. The moderator lifts his glass and says: "I drink this tea in mindfulness and gratefulness." Then we drink and eat in silence. We hear the sound of drinking and chewing; someone's stomach growls. We spend time together and share simple things. Tea, cookies, and our mindfulness.

Then we begin to share our experiences. Those we deem essential. Something joyful, something nourishing. We share stories, songs, and thoughts. We talk about our families, our work, our role models.

One of us speaks and the rest of us listen. They really listen. They don't interrupt. There is no distraction. We calmly follow our breath. A friend shared the observation that we built something akin to a common cathedral with this tea ceremony, we created a wide, social room, providing space for all that is. Another friend says that he hasn't experienced this form of community in over forty years. Some of us are touched.

Just a few cookies, some tea, and our mindfulness, and the small things are valued again.

The True Nature of Consumption

We Are the Chocolate

"May we only eat food that nourishes us and prevents illnesses." This is a line from the grace we say before meals in Plum Village. We are what we consume. We aren't separate from the object we consume. While we consume, we become one with the object of our consumption. It is not particularly hard to accept this insight. At first our senses get in contact with a product, then we physically reach for it, we chew it, and we swallow it. If we follow this process mindfully, we can see that the chocolate bar that sat in our drawer a little while ago is now moving through our blood. The thriller we watch in the movie theater enters our consciousness, sinks as memory into our store consciousness, and leaves traces in our everyday life. It becomes part of our experience. Whenever we make the decision to consume, we decide who we will be.

Bringing Light into the Darkness

Mindfulness connects us deeply with reality. When we turn our mindfulness toward products that we want to buy or consume, we try to see beyond their surface and recognize their true nature.

At no other time in history have humans had as much information about all the products we find in the supermarket as we have today. Yet it is still not easy to understand what we hold in our hands when we choose an item in the market. Even a small store might have up to 7,500 products, and in a department store there is exponentially more. At an average wholesale store we are confronted with 48,000 products. It is impossible to understand all these products completely. And beyond the sheer number of products, many products advertise themselves as something they are not.

Unambiguous Shopping Lists

Transparency needs engagement, time, and energy. Yet it is easier today on the internet. We can more easily find product information and connect with like-minded people. Facts about unwholesome and wholesome products travel faster around the globe. On a personal level, it might make sense to examine all the products we use in our household as a first step. With this list in hand, we assess all products we use according to their quality. What is good food, and what is bad food? Where is it difficult to make an informed decision? This list can help us develop more conscious consumer behavior. We should, however, beware of becoming ideological.

> *Plum Village, summer 2002. There is disagreement in the community about the politics of shopping. The Western monks are opting to buy 100 percent organic products, even if these cost twice as much. Many Vietnamese don't agree with this. They want to shop for less money and donate the savings to suffering children in Vietnam. Their argument goes further, saying that organic food products are also not affordable for more than half of the French population. Eating solely organic foods, therefore, would contradict the way of living simply.*

Witnessing this deep dispute about consumerism made an impression on me. It shows how important the deeper motivation of our shopping behavior can be. We can eat a fully organic diet based on purely egoistic motives. Or we can eat organic for the health of the planet, ourselves, and our community. We can eat cheaply in a mindless manner. Or we can consciously choose the cheapest foods in order to have more resources for other people. Our mental attitude while shopping might be more important than the organic asparagus in our basket. There is no need to delude ourselves.

Wholesome Products and Unwholesome Products

We need reliable basic information that allows us to know the true nature of a product. In meditation, this process is called "deep looking." We look at the true nature of an object without being distracted by its outer facade. What do we see? In many cases, we see how little we know. Often we do not know the origin of a product, how it was produced, who makes a profit off of it, or what the repercussions of the production are.

Consumers do bear this responsibility to consume consciously. It is not always easy to determine the quality of a product. And every one of us has a different understanding of what quality means. Does the product live up to its promise? How long does it last? Was it produced in a sustainable manner? Did people or the environment have to suffer during the production process? Were people or the environment exploited?

As a first step, it is important that we understand which of these criteria are meaningful to us. Again we need to work toward transparency. Consumer advice centers, test seals, product testing, and other strategies can help us. We can also sit together with friends and discuss our experiences. We can simply take ten household items, put them on the table, and ask what we know about them. What do we know about our children's stuffed animals, or our lightbulbs, dish detergent, T-shirts, flashlights, jeans, the flowers on the table, and our shoes? It is an exciting and informative process. The more we can define our criteria for shopping, the more we know about products, the stronger we can exercise our consumer power when we shop. Step-by-step we can comb through our household. Every shopping trip turns into a learning experience. When we act in this way, we reconnect with life, with the whole world, which flows through our lives in the form of products.

No product is perfect. Yet we can have an ideal that provides us with orientation and inspiration. A wholesome product is a product that has been produced in accordance with the five mindfulness trainings and is also consumed in that way. The product is the result of wholesome motivation and has been produced using wholesome methods. It came to us in a wholesome manner and its influence on our lives has a wholesome effect on our body and mind.

After a while, we begin to have a sense for more wholesome and less wholesome products. We begin to avoid the products whose origin or production process is not transparent. We also avoid those products that are produced in environmentally harmful and exploitative production processes.

In a world where economic processes are globally intertwined, it is increasingly difficult to understand individual products. An electric toothbrush might have one hundred individual pieces produced in twenty-three different countries. A car is even more complex. The closer we look into a product, the more we will know about its individual parts. We also need to be aware of the connection between cost and quality. Very low prices should give us pause rather than make us eager to buy.

Looking Deeply: Meat Consumption

The discussion about eating meat or refraining from eating meat is an emotional topic for many people. When I teach beginner seminars about mindfulness, I usually don't talk about the subject of eating meat or not eating meat, as it awakens resistance too easily. Here, however, I want to look into it extensively, because it is an example of our alienation from the consumption process. The discussion of "meat" makes many meat eaters feel uncomfortable because they easily feel accused. This is partially due to radical vegetarians who sometimes do attack in a moral and personal way and don't shy away from brutal confrontation. Here I want to do one thing only: take an unbiased look at the product "meat" and try to understand it more deeply in its interior and exterior interdependencies. What is the true nature of the meat we have on our plate? Where does it come from, how did it come into being, what are the effects of its production on the environment, what effect does it have on me when I consume it?

Consuming mindfully means that we watch every step of the production process with open eyes and decide to say: "Yes, I will eat this." With meat, however, this is difficult. The former owner of the big German meat market Herta, Karl Ludwig Schweisfurth, talks about his departure from the meat industry:

I have seen businesses with 1,000 pigs in an enclosure, animals vegetating in tight boxes. The pigs could hardly turn around and lie down on grate-like metal floors. Food is delivered by machines and excrement will automatically be flushed away. Doubt crept into my soul like lead.

These are the words of a professional butcher. What would happen to us if we visited these large-scale meat factories? The true nature of a slaughterhouse would most likely change our attitude about eating meat. The subject comes alive. The distance of the barrier between the counter in the butcher shop and the meat behind it is torn down. We make contact with the animals that will be slaughtered. We smell them, we hear them, and look into their eyes. Our experience with the origin of the meat becomes realistic, concrete, naked, and immediate. It will be killed. This living being that will be killed has emotions similar to ours—it is not quite as foreign to us as we might have assumed. The whole process leading up to the "final product" becomes clear and transparent. This need not frighten us. In a mindful economy it is important to shed light on these blind spots; it is important not to suppress and not to block them out. When we look closely and carefully at the meat industry, some of us might become vegetarians immediately.

From an intellectual perspective, there are also plenty of arguments against meat consumption. Many books have been written about the far reaching negative consequences of meat production. There are so many reasons to refrain from eating meat: deforestation of the rain forests for soy production, methane production from huge cattle herds, immense land usage (70 percent of all agriculturally used land serves the production of food for pasture-fattened animals), problems of manure disposal, and animal disease (which can also affect humans). This is just a brief summary, and we could argue extensively on each of these issues. After studying a variety of sources, I can summarize that current meat and fish production is one of the greatest catastrophes for our planet. Humankind can simply not afford continued meat consumption.

Yet there is another dimension. When we refrain from eating meat, we gain an excellent opportunity to cultivate compassion. Then we can overrule the separation between different degrees of respect for life.

After I started consciously forgoing meat, many things changed for the better in my life. I basically don't eat anything that I couldn't kill myself. I feel lighter in my body and in my mind. My body also changed. I lost weight. However, the greatest joy is that I feel more connected with all living beings.

I am aware how deeply meat consumption is rooted in our culture. And I do miss the favorite dishes of my childhood, like pork roast with red cabbage, meatballs, wiener schnitzel, and the Christmas goose. Sometimes I even do follow my impulses. Mindful consumption does not mean that we follow a catalog of rules and strive for perfection. But we should look with open eyes at the issue of eating animals.

How Do Products Die?

An unwholesome product can only emerge and survive if it is supported by a number of factors. A product is conceived by people; it is produced, transported, marketed, sold, and consumed. We are the economy. On each one of these levels, people have the chance to cross paths with a product and say: I am not going to nourish you, and I won't support you with my work.

If even one central condition ceases to exist, the product won't manifest any longer. It dies and will disappear from the shelves. A product will have a hard time surviving in the market when:

• Consumers refrain from buying it.

• Businesses refuse to offer it or delist it.

- A law is established to make the product illegal or tax it highly.

- Courts forbid it.

- Workers don't produce it.

- It is criticized in the media.

- Banks don't finance it.

- Professional organizations condemn its distribution.

- Product users are ostracized.

- The cost of the product is higher than its feasible market price.

We need courageous people who look deeply and disrupt the path of unwholesome products into the world on every level of the whole supply chain. We need the sales assistant who writes a letter to the executive board saying that they find it difficult to justify selling a harmful product day after day. And we need the media that refrains from accepting ads from certain producers or brands.

We can also phrase this positively: on every level of the supply chain we can encourage the production of wholesome products and services in our society: special credit options, state subsidies and tax exemptions, positive media coverage, and much more. Every one of us can contribute more energy to wholesome products.

We want to be able to understand what kind of impact a product has on ourselves and on the world. We don't deal with strangers we don't know. Before we make a connection with something, we want to be familiar with it. Before we support something, either by buying it or giving it our attention, we want to know what traces it has already left on our planet.

In other product sectors, it is easier. The closer we get, the more we know, the better we feel. When we know where an apple comes from, or even picked it ourselves, it "tastes" so much better than an anonymous product from the supermarket. We never eat just the apple!

Consumption of Generally Accepted Toxic Substances

On November 3, 2005, the German magazine *Der Stern* ran an article titled "How Healthy Is Alcohol?" I was flabbergasted at this title. It might be difficult to understand the effects of an electric alarm clock, yet is it really so difficult to understand the effects of alcohol consumption and alcohol abuse on ourselves and our society?

Some products subside in a fog, it seems to me. This makes it difficult to call them by their true names. Alcohol is one of the best examples of this phenomenon. Almost every single one of us has our own experiences with this drug. Most of us drink regularly or occasionally. I drank regularly, often way too much, starting in my teens and through my twenties. It seemed the most normal thing to me. At college, at home, at the companies I worked, during conferences and parties, at all of these occasions alcohol was taken for granted.

Thich Nhat Hanh says the following: "Some Buddhist teachers do not accept students who drink alcohol. I take a different approach. I don't say do not drink, but I ask that you may drink mindfully. When you drink in that way, it won't take very long until you stop drinking at all."

You might like to do the following exercise. Look at the illustration and think about the effects of alcohol in different areas of our society. What is the relationship between alcohol and violence? What effects does alcohol have on families? Write the effects and their impact along the corresponding arrow. You may want to choose additional dimensions. What is the result of your analysis? What does our deep search reveal?

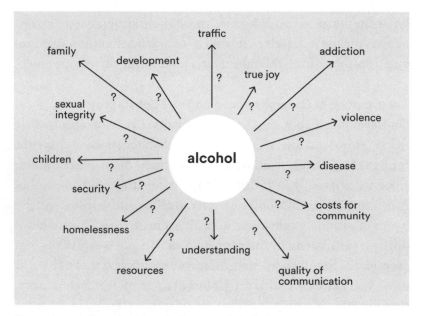

Illustration 22: Deep looking: the impact of alcohol

When we start to meditate, the negative effects of alcohol on our consciousness and clarity will become so obvious that it will seem absurd after a while to strive for mindfulness in our everyday life while we continue to drink alcohol. The deeper we look, the more clearly we recognize the unwholesome effects of alcohol in our environment.

Our consumption is never exclusively about ourselves. Maybe the seed of alcoholism is weak in us, yet strong in our partner or in our children. Maybe we can handle alcohol responsibly, but our friends and relatives might have difficulties. The effects of our own abstinence will radiate far beyond ourselves. Our friends and acquaintances will drink less in our presence. It is the most natural thing. Our encounters will be much clearer without alcohol.

Every Euro Counts

The sum of our consumption creates the economy that surrounds us. If we do not consume, there is no demand. Without demand, there is neither production nor supply. Our consumer decisions and habits determine the size and influence of every industry: the way chickens are bred, the subjects of researchers, the work conditions and wages in faraway countries. Consumers exercise an enormous power over the economy.

When a large number of consumers boycotts a company or a product, the product has no chance to survive. It will drop out of the market. Nothing survives without nourishment in the long run. Our consumption feeds products, companies, and jobs. When we choose to buy wholesome goods or services, we nourish the wholesome. When we buy unwholesome goods or services, we feed the unwholesome.

Consuming Mentally

In the field of material consumption, many organizations have started fighting for more transparency. This is wonderful. The collective consciousness is much more aware. Demand for sustainable products and brands is on the rise. The mental or spiritual dimension of consumption, however, doesn't receive much attention and is not very well understood yet.

Every year, the mental pollution of our environment increases. In the street, in the media, on the internet, and in stores, our mind faces a relentless stream of sensual impressions, ideas, images, and advertisements. All of these intend to stimulate our consumer habits. Consumption is much more than the simple purchasing of products. The media supplies us with multitudes of images and themes that occupy our minds and influence our moods. When we cultivate mindfulness, we become more aware of the vulnerability of our minds, and we realize that we have to protect ourselves when the economy is competing for our attention.

Detecting the Status Quo: An Analysis of Mental Consumption

For several years, I have been teaching an annual two-day seminar about the mindful handling of knowledge and information. The participants are usually academics who work in knowledge-intensive fields. At the beginning of the seminar, we conduct a mental input analysis. We ask ourselves which kinds of things we allow to enter our minds on a daily basis. Maybe you would like to follow along. Take all the time you need to complete the following table.

Input	Hours per week	Quality
TV		
radio		
newspapers		
magazines		
professional journals		
Internet		
DVDs		
movies		
theater and art		
phone / texting		
email		
listening to music		

In the second column, add the number of hours you spend consuming the respective stimuli per week. Take a regular week as your starting point. Many seminar participants count a total of between forty and sixty hours per week. They are shocked. They realize that they are constantly opening themselves to receiving stimuli.

In the third column, try to evaluate the subjective quality of the received inputs. You may assign between one and ten points.

Now we can begin our analysis. Where do I spend time with things that I don't value? Why do I allow so little time for something I find worthwhile? Which states of mind do I nourish? You can calculate how many years of your conscious life are spent with media consumption.

Now ask yourself: how much time do I spend on the conscious processing of all these impressions? How much time do I dedicate to meditation or contemplation? The next time we say that we have no time for meditation, we must remember this list.

Our list provides a clear starting point for making a change. We choose what we pay attention to and to what extent. We can go on a media fast. The more mindful we become, the less we allow harmful or time-wasting influences to enter our minds.

In Buddhist psychology, consumption is not merely restricted to the intake of outside impulses. The back -and-forth of our thoughts, emotions, and mental states produces our own nourishment. As we repeatedly think certain thoughts and indulge in certain feelings, we are the creators of our own world. As long as we don't see, don't understand, and don't influence this process, we have no agency. When we commit to color our days ourselves, be it positively or negatively, we hold the reins in our own hands.

What about Advertising?

Are you immune from advertising? I am not, not in the least. Advertising works. The more I meditate, the more I understand the subtle strategies that ads use. After spending a day exposed to billboards, commercials, and ad jingles, I can see these effects clearly. I feel more restlessness, desire, and discontent. Oftentimes these emotions are not clearly focused on a product or one subject, but they feed a prevailing mood that disturbs my happiness and clarity. Every commercial message that enters our mind colors it by a degree.

Buddhism stands by the clear maxim that our insight should be applied toward the benefit of all beings. We are supposed to help other human beings develop more wholesome mind-sets. Advertising as a field, however, takes a different approach. Advertisers use their psychological expertise to deliberately influence customers so they will act in the advertiser's interest.

This purposeful and professional exploitation of mental weaknesses and unwholesome mental states seems like mental abuse to me. The ninth mindfulness training of the Order of Interbeing states: "We will not spread rumors nor criticize or condemn things of which we are not sure." This statement is much more comprehensive than saying we will not lie.

Commercials rely on exaggerations, deceptions, and false promises and create a climate of communication that familiarizes us all too well with untruth. When we analyze posters, ads, and commercials in the media mindfully, we recognize the true nature of advertising. The greatest danger of advertising is that it nurtures and increases unwholesome mental states in our collective consciousness. These are states like anger, greed, discontent, fear, dishonesty, envy, and jealousy.

These mental states influence not only our purchasing decisions, but the whole manner in which we perceive our children, our partners, and our entire lives. Our mind is open and vulnerable. We need to learn how to protect it instead of participating in processes that increase confusion and dishonesty.

Protecting Our Mind and Our Senses
The Buddha's teachings say that we should look at our mind and body as a house with six open doors and windows. A steady stream of impressions enters our consciousness through our eyes, nose, ears, tongue, skin, and brain. The Buddha advised his students to examine carefully who and what they permit to enter their house.

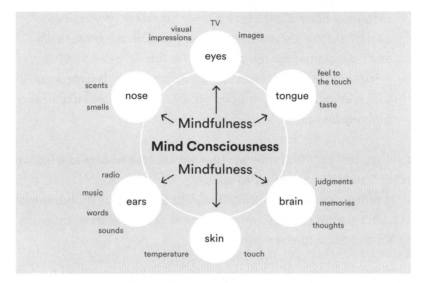

Illustration 23: Protecting our six senses

Mindfulness is the gatekeeper that helps us act more clearly. We can see with clarity:

- what we take in

- what kind of effect the object we consume has on us

- what benefits us and what harms us

We don't jump through every hoop that is set before us. The following story from the life of the Buddha serves as a teaching and an example for me:

One day, the Buddha was addressed by an angry priest who was full of envy and resentment because the Buddha's community was growing. He insulted the Buddha in many ways, accused him and yelled at him. The Buddha took it all in, remaining calm in body and mind. He did not react to the emotions of his accuser. After the storm of allegations had passed, a priest asked him in an

*irritated manner: "Why don't you say anything? Why aren't you
angry?" The Buddha countered: "Dear friend, if you give me a gift
and I refuse to accept the gift, who does this gift belong to?" The
priest said: "It belongs to me." The Buddha replied: "It is the same
with your anger. If I do not absorb it, it belongs to you and causes
suffering for you."*

Consuming mindfully means that we are free to decide what we
take in and what we refuse to take in.

Nothing can survive without fuel. The same is true for our mind.
If I don't give any energy and attention to certain ideas or thoughts,
they will be laid to rest over time.

Feeling the Dignity of Possessions

How do we deal with our new possessions after we have purchased
them? We tend to see ourselves as sovereigns over the objects we
acquire. We tend to think: this is *my* car, *my* tea kettle, *my* jacket. Our
apartments and houses are full of objects which we control, yet pay
relatively little attention to.

Zen practice encourages us to connect anew with these objects of
everyday life. We can breathe life into them again. When we pay a bit
more attention to our vase or tea pot, our car keys or our doormat,
when we pay some respect to them or award them a smile, we may
perceive the dignity of things.

Why don't you give it a try. Smile at the things you use on a daily
basis. Wipe the dust off some forgotten objects. Give away what you
don't have time to care for or don't need any longer. Unattended,
unnoticed objects steal energy. A household where everything has
its logical and assigned place radiates quiet clarity.

There is an Unlimited Supply of the Essential

The significant things in life, those that make life meaningful and
beautiful, are of an immaterial or spiritual nature. Love, meaning,

happiness, peace, joy, and contentment are of an immaterial nature. They cannot be purchased. Yet they are a daily nourishment for ourselves and for all of the people we interact with. David Suzuki writes:

> *Family, friends, community—these are the sources of the greatest love and joy that we can experience as human beings. We visit family members, stay in touch with our favorite teachers, share wonderful things with our friends. We take on difficult projects to help others, we save frogs or an idyllic nature spot, and as we do this, we experience a high sense of contentment. We find spiritual fulfillment in nature and by helping others. None of these joys requires material consumption, yet each of them is deeply fulfilling. These are complex joys and they take us much closer to true happiness than a bottle of Coke or our next minivan.*

Spiritual treasures are also infinitely available. We only need to touch them within ourselves and in others. The classical economic logic is rendered absurd when something so necessary is freely and infinitely available. When the essential cannot be found in the marketplace but within ourselves, classical economic ideas lose their meaning.

When we recognize that the most precious things in our lives are infinitely available and free of charge, we gain clarity, resolve, and courage to resist the daily promises of consumerism.

Consuming in Moderation

A Bit Less, Please!

When I was a child and my mother sent me to buy sausage and meat at the butcher shop, the saleswoman often put a bit more on the scale than I asked for. Instead of 200 grams, she might put 243 grams on the scale. Then she would smile and ask the standard question: "How about a little bit more?" I would say it was okay, of course.

I have never been asked in a store or in any other context: "How about a little bit less?" This question seems to be taboo in our society and economy. It is this question, however, that seems to be the only appropriate question right now with regard to consumer behavior.

"Could it be a little bit less?"

"Sure. It should be a bit less."

It is hard for us to find the right balance. There are so many examples: collective obesity, individual and collective debt overload, excessive media consumption, and so much more. We stick to the idea that an increase in consumption will also increase our happiness and reduce our problems.

Yet in many areas of our lives, an increase in consumption causes problems or creates a vicious cycle. We eat too much because we are frustrated, then we are frustrated because we gain weight. We fill our inner emptiness by consuming media, and solidify our solitude with this lonesome endeavor. We are annoyed by our boss and reward ourselves with a pair of new shoes after work. Then we are annoyed by the credit card bill that arrives a few weeks later. Frustration, loneliness, and anger cannot be reduced by consuming more.

In an affluent society, consumer impulses rarely arise from a material shortage but from a mentally perceived deficiency. We do not lack chocolate, cake, or beer, but we long for joy, contentment, and community. Consumption offers itself as a simple "solution." Many of us are very familiar with this mechanism. The poorer we feel, the more our mind asks for consumption. The less energy we have, the more we tend to grab these small, sweet promises and escapes.

Mindfulness helps me to refrain from seeking relief in consumerism. I have learned to look more closely at the causes underneath. I quietly breathe in deeply three times and tell myself with a smile: "What a clever consumer attack!" Most of the time, the consumer impulse cannot survive a direct confrontation and sinks back into the store consciousness.

How Much Do I Really Need to Eat?

When we eat quietly and with great concentration, we realize what is actually happening while we eat. This insight might come as a surprise to us. We sense the inner restlessness and impatience that fuels our eating habits. We see much more clearly what our true needs are. How much do we really need to eat? In economics, we talk about the principle of marginal utility. When we eat a plate of pasta five hours after breakfast, we will probably greatly enjoy it. If we eat a second plate, we might enjoy it less because we aren't nearly as hungry. If we eat a third or even a fourth plate, we might feel sick. We could even suffer from an upset stomach for the rest of the day.

We often eat so fast and so much that we do not notice the feeling of "Now I am full." It is only later that we realize "I ate too much." It is worthwhile to pay attention to that cycle. It is good to realize when we are full.

True Needs and Wrong Standards

Our lives have many more conveniences than those of historical rulers. We have access to goods from all over the world. From the perspective of the Middle Ages, we are immensely rich. Yet we don't feel that way. Why? We are governed by endless needs. On an individual as well as on a collective level, it is hard to accept our limits and to say: "This is enough. It is sufficient. I do not need more."

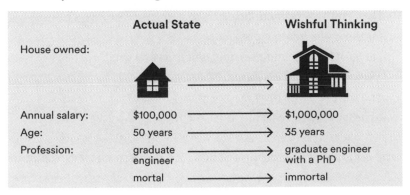

	Actual State	Wishful Thinking
House owned:		
Annual salary:	$100,000	$1,000,000
Age:	50 years	35 years
Profession:	graduate engineer	graduate engineer with a PhD
	mortal	immortal

Illustration 24: The wishes of Mr. P.

Thich Nhat Hanh teaches the following: "Nothing is more dangerous than to tie something that is limited to something without limits."

The limitless might be our desire for power, prestige, money, and sensual pleasure. The limited are our bodies, our time on earth, our energy. When limitless needs run into limited beings, we can be torn apart. We also put in danger the living conditions on our planet Earth, our home, with its limited resources. Endless desires, needs, hopes, expectations, entitlements, or dreams meet with a limited material world every day. Scientists estimate that if the whole world population consumed resources the way the Western world does, we would need between two and six planets the size of the earth to provide for everyone.[22]

There are natural limits to consumption, and we are closing in on the limit of our planet.

No More Agony of Choice

When Zsa Zsa Gabor, actor and icon of excessive consumption, was asked about her materialistic lifestyle, she said the following: "Whoever says that money doesn't make you happy has never been shopping." Zen Buddhism upholds a different teaching. In the famous poem "Xinxin Ming," Chinese Zen patriarch Seng-Ts'an teaches his students:

> *The Great Way is not difficult,*
> *for those who have no preferences.*
> *Let go of longing and aversion, and it reveals itself.*
> *Make the smallest exception, however,*
> *and you are as far from it*
> *as heaven is from earth.*

One could also say: comparisons and endless choices make us

---

22. New Economics Foundation and the Open University, *The UK Interdependence Report*, 2006, https://tinyurl.com/wlgkf8u.

restless and do not contribute to contentment and true happiness. If we are constantly asked to make choices, to compare and to pick the "best" option, we become exhausted and unhappy.

Researchers on consumer behavior looked at the connection between choices and emotional contentment. The maximizing of options, which is so often presented as an expression of freedom, does not increase our well-being. Many of us long for more simplicity.

Where Do We Stand?

What is too much for one person seems to be too little for another. Every human being has their own saturation point, and develops their own standard of living. Each human being is different and has different needs, related to health, age, family, and many other considerations. This is not about suggesting certain universal standards. I want to invite you, however, to reflect honestly upon your needs.

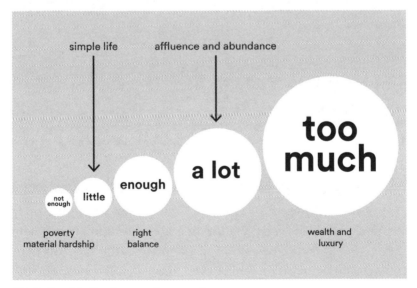

Illustration 25: Continuum of consuming

206 WE ARE THE ECONOMY

We can all agree that a continuum of consumption exists. We might disagree on setting the point of transition from right balance to affluence and from affluence to luxury. It can be worthwhile to exchange views with friends and family regarding the right balance.

It is always instructive to get to know people who have very different financial opportunities or consumer habits than we do. When millionaires meet the unemployed, it gets very interesting.

If we consider our whole life, we might detect big differences between people. One person might use all his income on cars; another one puts it into an apartment or travel. Here again we might ask whether we are on the middle path or verging on the extreme.

Dimension	too little	a little	enough	a lot	too much
Food					
Living					
Clothing					
Health					
Mobility					
Media					
Travel					

Table 7: Self-analysis on the right balance in different consumer dimensions

Letting Go of Luxuries

One of the first steps for monks and nuns when beginning their spiritual path is the renunciation of any material luxury. Usually they give away their possessions, and sometimes the handling of or contact with money is limited or even forbidden, depending on the strictness of the tradition of the order. The novices start a simple life. They focus solely on their essential basic needs while signaling to the outside world that true happiness cannot be achieved by material possessions or conveniences.

Our society is far from questioning material luxury. Every one of us dreams that we will be able to afford some of this luxury.

What speaks for giving up luxuries? Refraining from luxury is a clear sign that we want to focus on mental rather than material growth. It is an admission that our luxury is often only affordable at the cost of third parties. Luxury separates itself from the average. When we praise luxury or celebrate it at billionaire's galas, we admit that we believe ourselves to be entitled to more resources than others.

While luxury aims to encompass the unusual, the maximum, and the unsurpassed, the right balance is looking for reasonable solutions. These are solutions that can be realized for all, not just for a few, in a sustainable manner. A mindful economy does not strive for maximal quality, but more toward a reasonable balance, which is sufficient quality in all economic areas. In this way we create sustainable solutions and products for many instead of an exclusive minority.

As nice as the products that are designed by talented fashion creators and designers from all over the world might be, the fact of the matter is that they exude, by their exclusivity, the spirit of separation, exploitation, and envy. When we pay mindful attention, we understand that brands like Gucci, Hermès, Ferrari, or Louis Vuitton don't contribute much of anything that is helpful to the world.

It seems to be prudent to be more moderate in our wants both as individuals and as a society. Luxury has excessiveness woven into it.

Luxury is not harmless. While some people are building multi million-dollar villas, between 10,000 to 30,000 children starve every day, depending on how we make the calculation. This kind of inequality is very harmful. We are all in the same boat.

Most Western countries do not even manage to offer 0.7 percent of their gross national product (as suggested by the United Nations) to poorer countries. There are no legitimate arguments that justify our current lifestyle. We need to examine our own lives without sinking into shame, guilt, or helplessness.

The Middle Way

When we are confronted with the unjust distribution of wealth, we risk falling into the extreme of asceticism. We give everything away; we deny our needs and don't allow ourselves anything. We feel guilty when we indulge, and proud when we deny ourselves something. This is a false path. Thich Nhat Hanh writes: "It is important that we know our physical and psychological boundaries. We can't force ourselves into ascetic practices nor deny ourselves sensual pleasure. Right effort is found on the middle path between the extremes of self-denial and passionate sensual pleasure."[23]

A simple life has many advantages. Many people are surprised by how easy it is to get by with just a few things. It is astonishing that we rarely talk about the advantages of "less" in our society. There is even a feeling of fascination, liberation, and deep joy that comes with a decisive "Less!"

Upcycle Instead of Waste

In his famous book *Instructions for the Cook*, Dogen explains how a good cook should run the kitchen. They dedicate their attention to the smallest details. Their heart and all their mindfulness flow into the cooking process.

It is not just in the material aspect that we waste. We waste our collective mental health. We have allowed depression to become the most widespread disease of our time.

In a mindful economy, we will stop wasting our private and public resources, as well as our material and mental resources. We

---

23. Thich Nhat Hanh, *The Heart of the Buddha's Teaching.*

are looking for ways to save and reproduce resources. We want to appreciate our resources and increase their utilization factor. How can we change the collective throwaway mentality? Our model is a sustainable economic activity which does not eliminate a spiritual dimension.

Wastefulness needs to be understood, categorized, and addressed on all levels. Here are a few areas in which waste can be contained or stopped individually and collectively:

- waste of public goods that don't have a price tag

- waste of valuable raw materials in luxury products

- waste of end products by overproduction, scrapping of functionable products, and low utilization factors

- waste of labor by exclusion and discouragement of the unemployed and older people

- waste of wholesome mental states by unnecessary conflicts and a culture of separation

- waste by a lack of cooperation and unnecessary competition

- waste of community resources by individualization

- waste of mental energy by untamed thoughts, emotions, and mental states

These forms of waste are quite obvious. Certainly you can find other examples in your surroundings.

Are 174,720 Hours of Media Consumption Enough?

When is enough enough? It is important to consider this question. Above all it is important to answer this question in relation to our engagement with the media. No other consumer sector has managed to gain such a foothold in our day-to-day lives as the media over the last few decades. Today we consume more than eight hours of media per day on average. This includes the internet, daily newspapers, radio, professional journals, and also DVDs, movies, and music. Eight hours a day equals 56 hours per week, which is 2,912 hours per year and 174,720 hours in a lifetime in which this kind of consumer behavior is practiced for sixty years. This 174,720 hours equals thirty complete years of life in which we dedicate ourselves, besides eating and sleeping, exclusively to media consumption.

Every time I read these numbers, which are often confirmed by participants in my seminars about personal knowledge management, I am surprised all over again. Why do we open our minds voluntarily to so many films, music, news, images, crime shows, and advertisements? Why is it so much more likely to find someone engaged in some form of media instead of talking to someone else, or playing with children? There is no other area in which we have lost our balance as much as we have with media and entertainment.

One summer, I remember a boy came to the summer retreat in Plum Village. When he heard that there was no TV, he immediately wanted to go home. A nun told him: "Stay for one day, and if you are still bored, then you can go." The next day she asked him again. He didn't want to leave anymore. Why? He met children his age, and they had adventures in the woods nearby. The community made him alive again. He wanted to stay. His boredom disappeared. He didn't need the TV anymore. He had touched reality, and it was much more interesting than TV.

When surrounded by mindfulness, impulses for media consumption can subside in a natural way. Chain smokers don't miss their cigarettes. Passionate wine drinkers have tea and water. Information junkies calm down and turn their smartphones off. This is my experience from many mindfulness retreats.

Taming Our Mental Hunger

When we are hungry, we buy bread. That is fine. Oftentimes, however, the initial impulse for a consumer action is not as clearly defined as in the case of physical hunger. Our desire can be infinite, insatiable. In the sutra of the Eight Realizations of Great Beings, it says: "All hardships in daily life arise from greed and desire. Those with little desire and ambition are able to relax, their body and mind free from entanglement."

We all know the feeling of "This is all there is?" It can be a gnawing discontent that overcomes us in times of health and success. In Pali the word for this attitude to life is called *tanha*. *Tanha* is the root of all suffering. Unless we overcome *tanha*, we can't find lasting happiness. Yet *tanha* can't be overcome by consuming. The opposite is true: the more we feed our desire, the more powerful it becomes. The more we consume, the more we feed our consumer impulses.

In Buddhist mythology we find the image of the hungry ghosts. These are creatures with an enormous belly and a very narrow neck. They are always hungry, no matter how much food you offer them. It is never enough. Every one of us carries this never-ending desire inside, even though the objects that our hunger craves might be very different.

Our restlessness, our chase of new impressions and experiences, our fascination with the new and the boredom caused by the seemingly well-known, are variations of this universal hunger. Mindfulness can help us to distinguish between real hunger and *tanha*. If we stay mindful, we will see what we truly need.

Time to Fast, Time to Study

Phases of fasting are a good teacher on the path of finding the right balance. By conscious abstinence in central consumer areas, we recalibrate our input. Breaking our consumer habits and changing our lifestyle can help us to get in contact with a simple life. We can fast with food, alcohol, sweets, coffee, sex, shopping, or the media. Here, I want to emphasize the importance of media fasting for our mindfulness.

Media Fasting: Creating Space for Mental Digestion

Every stimulus we encounter we then need to digest so that we can integrate it meaningfully and harmoniously into our life. If we do not digest our food or swallow it without chewing properly, we create problems in our body. The same is true for our mind. If we take in too much information, too many opinions, images and theories, we don't have time to digest and to integrate these inputs into our lives. What good is an immense intake of inputs if I cannot use these to improve my life? Everything starts within the mind and we should actively place boundaries on what we take in. An especially effective method in this regard is media fasting.

Media fasting is the conscious refraining from ingesting media for a certain time. We can start with a balance sheet of our media intake, like the one we established at the beginning of this chapter. We can begin with the media that consumes most of our time and offers the least benefit to our quality of life. It waters only unwholesome seeds in our minds. We can make a commitment to refrain from or to limit the use of certain media for a period of time. We can also set an upper limit for our total screen time.

Reducing our media intake will result in a battle, similar to the effects of physical fasting. The mind will insist on the daily input of images, headlines, and emotional stimulation it is accustomed to. After the withdrawal, however, our mind has a chance to quiet down and time to clean up and recycle deposits of thought garbage. This detoxification creates a more alert consciousness.

The fast has to fit into our current life situation. It makes no sense for a reporter to refrain from using his phone in the middle of finishing a story.

After a media fast, the consumption of media usually shrinks quite a bit. We recognize our impulses more clearly and decide more consciously about our information needs. Fasting wakes our desire for real contact with the world. Secondhand realities seem increasingly unattractive. Many people experience phases of fasting as cleansing, and they become a starting point for finding a more suitable balance. In a spiritual context, fasting is a conscious decision "to be nourished by something else," to give priority to the spiritual or mental dimension.

Taking Our Time

Many people tell me that they do not have time for meditation or other mindfulness practices. Their days are too busy, too scheduled. This may be true. Yet our constant busyness does not exist in a vacuum. It is the logical consequence of many of our previous decisions. We cram too much into our days: we have too many leisure-time activities, we have too many wishes, too many duties, too much work. The more we have, the more we do; the more we buy, the more energy we need in order to finance it all, to take care of it all, to plan, to coordinate, and so on. This keeps us continuously running.

This dilemma creates a paradox: we constantly acquire more, yet we can't enjoy what we have more of. We need more time to digest and to turn inward. We have a tremendous amount of treasures in our storehouse. Let's take the time to enjoy these. Let's pause and look at our riches. Let's not constantly run around and try to find more spectacular things outside that we can acquire. Let's settle into our storehouse. Let's make it into our home. Thich Nhat Hanh invites us to say: "I have arrived. I am home."

To arrive in the present moment means that we clearly see the treasures that we already have. We shouldn't sacrifice the present for the future. It is possible to touch our interior and exterior treasures in every moment anew. Then our friends, our spouses, our children, our parents, and everything in our lives will be livelier and more precious.

When we recognize our true needs, we can relax. I have watched many people blossom in very simple conditions in an atmosphere of mindfulness. We need compassion, mindfulness, brotherhood and sisterhood; we need contentment, trust, and joy. These are true needs. They deserve priority. Let's get rid of dead freight so we can take care of them.

The Motivation of Consumption

Understanding Our True Motivation for Consuming

What triggers our consuming? What do we expect from our consumption? We should look carefully and understand what it is that causes our consumption and accelerates it. We should recognize the influences that significantly affect the amount of our consumption:

- Is it simple habit?

- Is it a societal norm that we follow?

- Are we following a fashion or a trend?

- Is contact with friends, neighbors, or experts triggering us?

- Do we have certain ideas of happiness?

- Are these opportunities we can't resist?

- Is there an irresistible urge or an addiction?

- Are we comparing ourselves with others who have more?

- Do we buy something to reward ourselves?

- Do we want to be liked by others?

- Do we identify with the object of our purchase?

- Did we lose control?

• Was it a reasonable and carefully considered decision?

Our consumer decisions are rarely conscious, rational, smart, or completely independent. Many of our buying decisions happen emotionally and unconsciously. The motivation for these decisions is not always easy to decipher for us.

Why do we no longer like the shoes that we deemed perfect for us two years ago? Why do we feel that our apartment is too small and we need a bigger one? What is it that motivates us to think this way?

Do we have a beer because we are thirsty? Do we reach for the newspaper because we want to read about the news of the day? Do we make decisions in a clear and conscious manner? The longer we practice mindfulness, the more clearly we begin to see that our seemingly free and conscious decisions are not actually so free and conscious. We let a lot of them happen to us. The below illustration shows the variety of conscious and unconscious consumption accelerators in our lives.

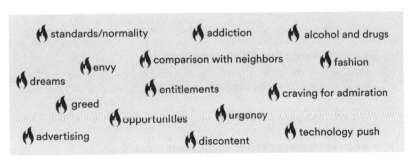

Illustration 26: Interior and exterior consumption accelerators

All of these triggers make a promise to us: Follow me and it will be pleasant. Don't follow me and it will be unpleasant. These promises waft around us like winds in our day-to-day life.

Calming the Eight Winds

In Buddhism, we call these promises and threats the eight worldly winds. They are gain and loss, honor and disgrace, praise and criticism, happiness and unhappiness.

We would rather win than lose, rather be praised than reprimanded, rather be admired than despised, and rather experience pleasant than unpleasant sensations. Consciously and unconsciously, we work hard to experience the pleasant or hold on to it and to keep the unpleasant at bay or push it away.

We pursue the pleasant and feel happy when:

- we receive money and material possessions

- we receive praise or approval

- when we enjoy a good reputation or image

- when we enjoy pleasant images, sounds, scents, tastes, and touch

We run into the unpleasant and feel displeasure and resentment when:

- we lose money and material possessions

- we receive criticism, objection, and disapproval

- our reputation is damaged

- when we are exposed to unpleasant images, sounds, scents, tastes, and touch

When we lay out our motivations and responses in this way, the source of suffering is made clear. When we personally experience this insight, the eight winds will calm around us.

Addiction: Source of Dependence
Addiction starts when we can no longer decide freely to do

something or to refrain from doing it. Addictions can destroy our body, our family, and our financial livelihood. Above all, they destroy our spiritual development as a human being. They force us into destructive mental and physical repetitions. With every repetition of our addiction-driven behavior, we die a little bit. When you enter the cycle of addiction, you begin to destroy yourself and your surroundings.

Addiction has many faces. Some addictions are despised (heroin, for example), while others are socially accepted, even honored and rewarded. Addiction to success, addiction to work, and addiction to consumption are strong accelerators of our economy. Yet addiction is addiction. Addiction is an escape. Addiction is dependence. Joko Beck writes: "Underneath all the seeking we find sorrow."

Our constant seeking and busyness may be a sign that we are not able to or don't want to turn toward the truly essential. Addiction in its many forms has become normal in our society. What drives us into addiction? The Buddha answered this question clearly and deeply. As human beings we desire pleasant experiences. We strive for enjoyment. Nice weather, a relaxing bath, intimate sexuality, or a good meal. Upon first glance, it seems to be a good strategy to maximize the pleasant experiences and to avoid the unpleasant ones.

This behavior of avoidance, however, is the gateway into addiction. It gives our emotions enormous power over us. The more we avoid, the less freedom we have. Addiction can come in all different forms. The fewer unpleasant feelings we can tolerate, the more dependent we become on that which can provide us with pleasure. It is only during withdrawal that we confront all of our physical and mental pain and problems. A sound mindfulness practice can strongly support withdrawal from addictions of any kind.

Recognizing and Transforming Consumer Habits

We do not give much thought to many of our consumer decisions. They occur more or less automatically. Our life, however, is not a repetition. Everything we do repeatedly has the tendency to strengthen, to harden, to solidify, and then more and more to run mechanically. Everything can become a habit: the way we plan what to do in our free time, how we brush our teeth, and how we exercise. This applies of course to our consumer habits as well.

Our inner freedom begins when we no longer accept the normal as "normal" any longer. Habits aren't static. They are a powerful pattern of energy. They attract actions. They are like a parched riverbed where fresh water finds its preferred pathway after a downpour. Mindfulness has the power to make our habits visible. We can scrutinize the "normal."

We should not perceive our bad habits as enemies. We do not need to fight and destroy them. Every inner struggle nourishes our restlessness and aggression unnecessarily. Every struggle feeds our habits additional energy instead of weakening them. Let us handle our habits gently. Let us name them appropriately and smile at them forgivingly. They are old acquaintances. They have been with us for so long. May they die in peace.

Every habit requires certain conditions in order to manifest. Nothing can survive in the long term without nourishment. No birds, no company, no process, no product, and no habit. In order to make coffee we need a coffeemaker. When we don't have chocolate at home, we can't indulge our hunger attack at midnight. When our smartphone is on silent, it can't disturb us during a conversation. Only when we are online can we be reached by email impulses and relent to constant interruptions. It is up to us to create an environment that makes it harder for consumption impulses to find nourishment and strengthen themselves.

Finding Refuge in the Wholesome

Where do we turn when we are feeling bad? Where do we resort to when the wind is blowing into our faces and we do not know what to do? In times of anxiety, insecurity, and strong emotions, we need something to hold on to. Do we find refuge with our families, with friends, in God? Where is a safe place?

True refuge is a safe place where we can regenerate, where we can sort out and understand our situation. We showed that our consumption cannot offer us this safe place.

In Buddhism we know the threefold refuge of the Buddha, the dharma (the teachings that help us to awaken), and the sangha (the community that supports us on our path). A dharma teacher I practiced with summarized this type of refuge in the following way:

> We trust that we may understand reality deeply and overcome our unnecessary suffering just as the historical Buddha did. We have a precise role model to show us how to master spiritual crises. We trust in the many methods of Buddhist teachings, which we test in our own life with the help of proven practice methods. We trust in the community that helps us learn and supports us in difficult times with advice and encouragement. And we trust in our own practice. Instead of seeking refuge in the outside, we return to our mindful breath and realize without judgment what is going on in our body and mind. We take a few mindful steps and read the five mindfulness trainings to connect our life with something beautiful and truthful. There is a place that is full of peace and quiet that no one can take away from us.

Tibetan monks who survived torture in Chinese prisons without spiritual or physical detriment were asked about their greatest fears during imprisonment, and how they preserved their mental integrity. Their greatest fear was to lose compassion for their tormentors and turn to hatred and anger instead. They were sure that seeking refuge in unwholesome mental states would have destroyed their lives. They decided to find refuge in the wholesome instead of the unwholesome.

We can take refuge in television, alcohol, and food, or we can decide to choose deep listening, meditation, and deep looking. We may seek refuge in negative thoughts or in kind well wishes. We can see the negative or the positive in others. Every moment we decide anew which view of the world we will hold dear.

We Are the Future

Once we let go of our wrong perceptions regarding happiness and success, we can lead a free and happy life. Many of us do not feel free. We feel that we do not have a choice and are servants to huge economic structures. We are looking for alternatives. We need to cultivate our freedom.

I am so grateful for mindfulness practice and my teachers that led me out of the prison of false perceptions. We have many choices. We need to see them, however, and then act decisively. The prerequisite, for me, was to commit to a regular daily practice that keeps me present and aware in my day-to-day life. Whatever I cannot see clearly, I cannot change.

Mindfulness practice works. When I founded the Network for Mindful Business in 2003, I had only a vague idea of how to bring awareness, ethics, and meaning into the economy. Today, I see this path more clearly.

There is a growing dissatisfaction with the ways we organize our economy and how we think about it. Over the years, I have met many entrepreneurs, managers, business consultants, professors, and financial experts who are looking for new answers and perspectives regarding our economic system. We need to overcome paralysis, anger, and helplessness in order to develop joyful and pleasant energy together. Intellectual insights are not enough. We need to become the change that we want to see among us. Otherwise our voices will not be strong enough. The credibility and inspirational power of a person depends on how much they succeed at reflecting their ideas in their own ways of living.

Let's start with changing ourselves. Then we will be able to send meaningful impulses to companies, universities, and political processes. Let us not deceive ourselves. We cannot force ourselves to be more mindful, more ethical, more compassionate and understanding than we really are. We need to develop and master patience. The patient cultivation of mindfulness will show us how to act in a meaningful way. The best investment we can make as human beings is in our own minds. Cultivating wholesome mental states, taming unwholesome mental states, and looking deeply into our own life situation will lead us to a freer, kinder, and more meaningful life.

Daily Practice in Our Own Household
When we anchor mindfulness by methods like walking, sitting, eating, and work meditation, and deepen our practice by studying, and attending retreats and mindfulness days, we begin to change our own household step-by-step and without any false ambition. What do we buy, and where do we buy? Is this the right bank for us to keep our money in? What purposes should our money serve? How do I create time for deep breathing during my work processes? These are practical questions, and it is joyful to answer these with concrete actions and experiments. When we allow mindfulness to be our teacher, our learning process will be an easy one. We can see the path that we must follow clearly. Yet we also see that there are no easy answers.

In the Plum Village tradition, the Buddhist tradition of Thich Nhat Hanh, the community—the sangha—is very important. There are more than 1,000 groups in the Plum Village tradition worldwide that support each other in their daily practice and their spiritual growth. They tend to meet weekly for practice evenings. Our habits are strong. Community helps us to stay involved and not to abandon the path.

We do not need to become Buddhists to practice mindfulness. We can stay rooted in our Christian, Jewish, Muslim, humanist, or other traditions and deepen our insights through mindfulness. Many of my ordained Buddhist friends are still active and at home in their Christian and Jewish communities.

Attending and Organizing Mindfulness Days

As a first concrete action, I recommend attending a mindfulness day. A mindfulness day is a powerful entry into and an effective deepening of our mindfulness. I am always touched to see how much we can learn during such a day, both about ourselves and about others. Without effort, our central beliefs and our habits are made clear. It is good to indulge ourselves in such days of pausing. They offer high-quality mental nourishment, give our body and mind calm and clarity, and let us spend time with like-minded people who inspire us. Mindfulness days are an effective medicine and a healing fertilizer for our society. A sample mindfulness day might look like this:

until 9:30 am	Arrival and tea
9:30 am	Welcome
10:00 am	Introduction to mindfulness practice
10:15 am	Sitting meditation, walking meditation
11:15 am	Break
11:30 am	Dharma talk
12:45 pm	Mindful lunch
2:30 pm	Walking meditation in nature
3:15 pm	Leisure time
4:00 pm	Mindful exchange
5:15 pm	Short sitting meditation
5:30 pm	Evaluation
6:00 pm	End of the day

It is important to make tried-and-true methods of mind training more widely accessible to all levels of society. It would be wonderful if more and more people from all sectors of society had the opportunity to personally experience mindfulness practice.

Making an Impact in Society

Our desire and readiness to share our experiences with others grows as our mindfulness becomes stronger and our insights clearer. We can start meditation groups in the office; we can integrate mindfulness into our lessons or talks; we can suggest more effective communication strategies among our teams or organize a mindfulness day for friends and coworkers. There are so many ways to get started, and every one can start right where they are. It is easiest when we join with like-minded people, even if it is just one friend. In the United States, there are three monasteries in the Plum Village tradition that are open to everyone: Deer Park Monastery, in Southern California; Blue Cliff Monastery, in New York; and Magnolia Grove Monastery, in Tennessee. You can visit for a day of mindfulness, or stay for a weeklong retreat.

This book is a first step. Our experiences in the field of mindful economics will continue to grow. The world's economic order will change. Openness toward new economic concepts that will integrate true mental development will grow. As more and more people cultivate mindful economic practices in their own lives, more organizations will manifest these practices and breathe mindfulness. It will be a joy to work in these places.

Maxims of Mindful Economic Action

May we see the economy as an adaptable, influenceable process rather than a rigid, unchanging law of nature.

May we be able to connect with others through our work, our money, and our handling of money rather than be separated from them.

May we stay in touch with the present rather than getting lost in the future, caught in the past, in constant busyness or in stress.

May we nourish all that is wholesome within ourselves and in our surroundings.

May we constantly honor and appreciate anew all things, no matter how small and inconspicuous.

May we learn to live in balance.

May we protect our mind mindfully.

May we watch our present state of mind and cultivate distance to impulses.

May we appreciate the world of fullness rather than construct a world of shortage.

May we choose a wholesome and supportive environment.

May we nourish our mindfulness, joy, and compassion on a daily basis.

―――

May we learn to give without expecting to receive.

May we experience gratitude on a daily basis.

May we let things ripen and practice patience.

May we feel the joy of simple living.

May all beings be happy.

We are the economy—and so much more.

Blessings for you and for our path.

Acknowledgments

This book has many fathers and mothers. It is a collective manifestation. Without my teachers, my family, my sangha, my fellow
travelers and friends, this book could not have been written. My
wife, Bettina, supported me with her love (her love for the dharma
and for me) and inspiration to keep writing and stay the course. Her
kind feedback during the writing process saved me from stress and
phases of creative blockage. My son, Jonathan, is a true adventurer.
His joy, freshness, and beginner's mind showed me the way again
and again.

I am grateful to my teacher Thich Nhat Hanh for a vivid transmission of the Dharma, which he himself embodies in such a beautiful
way. May his wisdom continue to radiate strongly into the world.
Barack Obama showed me that the seeds of wisdom can sprout in
all areas of life, in politics and in economics. I wish him success
and support in his efforts promoting openness, understanding, and
inclusivity. This book is dedicated to Thich Nhat Hanh and Barack
Obama. May wisdom and power walk hand in hand.

My friends and network companions Christian Kobler, Ilsalbe
Sachs, Markos Arnold, Max Biller, Michael Heidecker, and Stefan
Pinter commented on the completed manuscript. Thank you so
much for your insight and open words. I want to thank my editor
in Germany, Nadja Rosmann, for her relaxed and flexible coordi-
nation of the production process, her professional input and (in
hindsight) for her stoic insistence on the agreed book length (which
made me delete more than 400,000 cherished characters). I met

many people during the last ten years who left their mark on this book, and supported and encouraged me in many different ways. My thanks goes to: Alex Barkawi, Annabelle Zinser, Annette Saager, Arnd Bätzner, Burghard Lippke, Christian Bergmann, Christoph Bründl, Claas Wenzlik, Franz Katzlinger, Fumon Nakagawi Roshi, Georg Lolos, Gertraud Czerwenka-Wenkstetten, Gesine Buss, Grit Turnowsky, Günter Hudasch, Helmut Hallier, Hermann Küster, Holger Moller, Jan Erhardt, Joachim von der Goltz, Karin Haider, Karl Schmied, Lutz Tornow, Manfred della Schiava, Marcel Geisser, Marianne Woide, Martin Schaurhofer, Mathias Köhl, Munish Schiekel, Nel Houtman, Peter Ducret-Novak, Thomas Eberle, Rainer Pallaske, Reinhard Wilfort, Richard Pircher, Rudi Passawa, Sascha Spoun, Seon Kwang Haengja, Sister Chau Nghiem, Sister Jina, Stephan Ludwig, Susanne Kunz, Tenzin Droelpa, Thay Doji, Thay Phap An, Thay Phap Thanh, Ursula Hanselmann, Ursula Richard, Waltraud Pichler and Wendelin Küpers.

I am grateful to my parents, Ellen and Peter Romhardt, for their continuing and caring support of our family.

The following institutions supported and inspired me over many years in my work: Buddhistische Akademie Berlin-Brandenburg, Danube University Krems, Österreichische Buddhistische Religionsgemeinschaft (Austrian Buddhist Religious Community), the Order of Interbeing, Plum Village, Quelle des Mitgefühls (Sangha in Berlin), Sangha Zehlendorf, Schweizerische Gesellschaft für Organisation, the German Academic Scholarship Foundation, and the University of St. Gallen. Special thanks also to the bonanza coffee heroes, the St. Oberholz, the Hotcafé at Mutter Courage, Starbucks at Teltower Damm, and Bolles Bootshaus at the beautiful Wannsee.

I owe a lot to the experiences of many unnamed members of the Network for Mindful Business, who helped me to gradually study the deeper dimensions of our economic activity. Thank you for your sharing, your friendship, your courage, and your *dana* that made this book possible.

Finally, I am grateful to all teachers of the dharma who inspired me by their way of living, teaching, and writing. Besides Thich Nhat Hanh, I want to give special thanks to Bernard Glassman, Jack Kornfield, Jon Kabat-Zinn, Joko Beck, Joseph Goldstein, Larry Rosenberg, Mahathera Henepola Gunaratana, Pema Chödrön, Sawaki Roshi, Shunryu Suzuki, Sogyal Rinpoche, and Thubten Chödrön. Each has shown me wonderful ways that we can change the internal and external world for the better.

The Network for Mindful Business

The Network for Mindful Business (Netzwerk Achtsame Wirtschaft) was founded in 2004 in Berlin. The network is a nonprofit and dharma-based community of practitioners. We explore new ways of undertaking wholesome business activities together, starting with ourselves. We support each other on the path toward increasing compassion, freedom, and understanding.

We organize around 160 events each year in the German-speaking world: retreats, seminars, mindful coworking days, impulse evenings, public walking meditations, and more. The network is currently active in eighteen cities, including Berlin, Vienna, Frankfurt, and Hamburg.

We see business and the economy as powerful forces that shape our societies and want to explore wholesome attitudes and actions that may lead companies, organizations, leaders, and others on a mindful and compassionate path in all kind of business-related action and thinking. We see mindfulness not as a tool but as an essential part of the Eightfold Noble Path, the Seven Factors of Awakening, and other precious teachings of the Buddha.

We were founded by friends in the Plum Village Dhyana tradition of Thich Nhat Hanh and cherish these roots, but we are open to the insights of other Buddhist and contemplative traditions. Our ethical ground is defined by the Mindful Business Commitment, and the Fourteen Mindfulness Trainings of the Order of Interbeing.

In 2019, we decided to offer our experiences in English on a broader scale, and to invite people around the world to connect with us: https://achtsame-wirtschaft.de/naw-join-us.html.

About the Author

Kai Romhardt is a Buddhist Dharma Teacher in the tradition of Plum Village. He works as a speaker, author, lecturer, retreat leader, trainer, and coach. In his first career, he worked as a management consultant and scholar in the field of knowledge management. He also worked for a short period as a consultant at McKinsey & Company. Kai has authored seven books on management, organizations, and the various aspects and impacts of mindfulness on our life, work, and thinking.

At the age of thirty-one, Kai experienced a deep identity crisis that led him to Buddhism and to Plum Village, where he spent two years living, studying, and practicing under the guidance of Zen Master Thich Nhat Hanh. He received ordination in the Order of Interbeing in 2002 and received Dharma lamp transmission from Thich Nhat Hanh in 2010.

After his return to Germany, he settled in Berlin and started the Network for Mindful Business in 2004. He also started Sangha Zehlendorf with his wife, Bettina.

 **PARALLAX PRESS**

Parallax Press, a nonprofit publisher founded by Zen Master Thich Nhat Hanh, publishes books and media on the art of mindful living and Engaged Buddhism. We are committed to offering teachings that help transform suffering and injustice. Our aspiration is to contribute to collective insight and awakening, bringing about a more joyful, healthy, and compassionate society.

For a copy of the catalog, please contact:

Parallax Press
P.O. Box 7355
Berkeley, CA
94707

parallax.org